MINISTERING
IN THE PAULINE CHURCHES

Ministering
in the Pauline Churches

Pheme Perkins

PAULIST PRESS
New York/Ramsey

Library of Congress
Catalog Card Number: 82-60849

ISBN: 0-8091-2473-4

Published by Paulist Press
545 Island Road, Ramsey, N.J. 07446

Printed and bound in the
United States of America

Contents

Introduction

No one can deny that we live in a time of change and even turmoil over the role and style of religious leadership. The activism of the 1960's has left an uneasy legacy. Christians no longer presume that the institutional arrangements of the Church are a reflection of the Gospel. Indeed, they have seen those arrangements change with enough frequency to wonder if they are even written in so stable a medium as sand. Christians are painfully aware of the complex relationships between Church and social and political structures. They know that that entanglement may serve to legitimate oppression and persecution. They also see Christians painfully divided over their response to such situations. Christians cannot pretend that the same questions about equality, justice and freedom that press upon them in the global and national arena are of no significance for the Church.

Of course, the majority of Christians only reflect upon the dramatic issues which are covered in the press. We hear about the formation of "basic communities" in Latin America and of clergy and lay workers involved in a struggle against oppressive governments so that the poor can have food and land. At home, we hear the demands of women, married people and others for equality within the Church. We watch the struggle over the ordination of women and homosexuals in various denominations. We hear of Roman Catholic women who refuse to accept exclusion from sacral ministry. Some defy bans

1

against being lectors, preaching and even celebrating the Eucharist. Other women, less publicized, are leaving the Roman Catholic Church for communions in which they will be able to exercise an ordained ministry. Some Roman Catholic men who wish to marry are following similar routes. A conservative element within the Roman Catholic Church says: "Good riddance." They even expect that the Roman Catholic Church will be able to settle back into the pre-1960's stability that some remember and others only romanticize.

Such dreams fail to recognize what has happened to the Roman Catholic Church in the past two decades. Vatican II showed us that the Roman Church was no longer "Roman." The issues raised by the North American and European Catholics may even have to give place to the global concerns coming from those in third world countries. The Latin American struggle for "basic communities" cannot be swept away as deviant regionalism. It concerns us all, since we are all part of a global order which affects the very lives of those people.[1] The African churches may much more reasonably press the claim for a married clergy. Groups who owe their existence and their Christian faith to married, lay catechists seek to have such persons serve them as ordained ministers.[2] Bishops from third world countries raise even more pressing questions about how the universality of the Roman Catholic Church is to be expressed. Need universality imply uniformity in liturgical praxis, in sensitive moral areas like marriage and birth control, in symbolic expressions of doctrine? Or does uniformity simply serve to advance the hegemony of European culture over the rest of the world?

We are not about to engage in advocating a solution to such complex questions. However, the very questions themselves attest an important shift in consciousness among Christians. J. Metz has described this shift as the coming of a new, adult maturity among Christians. The paternalistic Church in which clergy cared for a flock, which was always religiously immature and unable to discern religious or moral issues, the Church of a colonialism in the mission, is passing away. So, too, is the individualistic Church of the post-Enlightenment West. That approach to Church sees the clergy as dispensing a service which the private individual may or may not incorporate into the individual pursuit of happiness. The Church is one among many "self-help" or private enlightenment movements. It is there to make me feel good, to help with times of personal crisis, to sanctify transitions in life. The individual, on the other hand, stands rather aloof from the Church. It has no right to make demands on him or her unless those demands fit into the project of self-improvement the individual chooses to pursue, like weight watchers meal plans. Such individualists often treat the Church as they do the government. They become irate and vocal when they do not find such institutions providing the services they require. Yet they do not have the willingness to involve themselves in the community and its needs.[3]

Both immature forms of Church permit variations on the clergy/laity division. The paternalistic father/child relationships of the first type are simply replaced by the authoritarianism of a professional class against the "non-expert" typical of a technological society. Two forms of reaction against such domination are also part of our experience. On the one hand, non-ordained persons can attain the same or even greater expertise in all the disciplines relevant to ministerial activity. (Or, conversely, clergy seek professional degrees to make their status hold.) The churches no longer have exclusive control over the sources of such expertise, since most of the required information and even important advances are made in universities and not seminaries. On the other hand, those who are well-educated but not experts in particular fields have been pressing to take some of the territory back from the experts, whether in law, medicine or religion. Used to being "experts" in a particular field, they demand equivalent treatment in others.

Both the availability of expertise in theology, counseling, liturgy, community development and the like to non-ordained Church members and the growing demand among the populace that expertise serve and not dominate others are important to developing the third type of community. Such a community will not perceive "the Church" as a property belonging to clergy and religious into which the rest of us are occasionally admitted or a professional service rendered by clerical or other experts whose dictates have the force of binding revelation. Instead, all members of the community are responsible for its well-being and survival. That responsibility implies that those members are also to be accorded a voice in what sort of community they have. Like it or not, such a community will have to learn lessons of pluralism, consensus and compromise.[4] How religious communities can best reach such a consensus still remains a difficult problem. E. Braxton has suggested a complex process of community reflection which would respect the various roles and authorities within the community and yet assure that the positions held by that community articulate the experience of all its members. Otherwise, the transforming power of our religious symbols is lost. They become markers in an intellectual game, which few play with any passion or commitment.[5]

Christians find that they do not have to invent such a new community out of whole cloth. It corresponds more closely than either the paternalistic or the "private enlightenment" Church to the realities of Christian community in the formative period. We must constantly correct our vision in reading the New Testament. Its comments on community and authority are inevitably read through the "clergy (experts)/others" division that has characterized so much of Church life. Yet that dualism did not exist. Neither Jesus nor the apostles qualified as "priests" in any of the senses that were culturally available in their world.[6] When he was a Pharisee, Paul might have qualified as a religious expert of sorts, but he tells us that all of that became garbage when he came to know Christ (Phil 3:8–11). "Apostolic authority" appears as the struggle for a new form of authority in a new type of religious community. Not surprisingly, we find that experiment charged with uncertainty, even dissension. But such a community could not come into being without trying for new forms. The various images available in the culture did not serve.[7]

New forms of authority and community also required forms of ministry and responsibility for that community which were not always easily understood. Today, Christians recognize the Pauline combination of a wide diversity of gifts used for the service of the one community as a powerful image of their own quest for a more genuinely adult Church. This picture presents us with gifts of the Spirit which cannot be regimented either into clerical/non-clerical spheres of responsibility or into fields in which some persons might hold the power of expertise. To attempt to regiment what is to count as a call of the Spirit to build up the community into some administrative category might even represent the height of audacity.[8] At the same time, Paul experienced the divisiveness, lack of charity and, perhaps, outright scandal that could develop in a community which did not perceive that such gifts are not for personal aggrandizement. They must always serve the unity and building up of the larger community. Unity is a persistent theme in Paul's development of the diversity of spiritual gifts.[9] Increased diversity and pluralism within the Church can only be the manifestation of the Spirit as it contributes to the well-being and the unity of the whole. Despite the panic which the great flowering of diverse ministries creates in some circles, it may be possible to see that these gifts are more than a desperate "stop gap" for a lack of clergy. Instead, they may be seen as appropriate contributions to the unity of the Church. They help to overcome the "irrelevance" of Church as a clerical preserve by bringing more and more members of the community to have a personal stake in the well-being of the Church. Adult Christians cannot pass off the blame for failures in their Church or their faith to someone else if they are unwilling to accept the possibility that the Spirit requires some form of service from them. Adult Christians cannot pass judgment on the attempts of others to discern the signs of the Spirit without recognizing that the same judgmental attitude may condemn their own projects. As Paul quickly found with the Corinthians, believers may have a harder time loving each other than they do loving the outsiders. He reminds them that those who fail to "discern the Lord's body in the community" are liable to the same judgment God will pass against unbelievers (1 Cor 11:17–34).

The following chapters are not an exhaustive treatment of ministry in the New Testament. They originated in requests from three different groups for lectures during August and September 1981. In all cases, the audience was largely persons who were not members of the clergy but who were engaged in various forms of ministry and religious education. The organizers of the various meetings suggested the topics that would be of concern to their audience. The lively interest and discussion which followed all of the presentations persuaded me that I should prepare the material for publication. As those with tapes or copies of the original lectures will recognize, they have been extensively rewritten. I trust that the present version reflects something of the conversation and exchange of experiences that took place both formally and informally with the groups involved. They represent the "wisdom community" out of which this material has emerged.

All of the materials developed here are centered on the

Pauline communities, though some treatment of other examples in the New Testament is given. Ministry is best documented for the Pauline churches, since the apostle provides information about them in his letters. The first three chapters on evangelization, worship and the role of women were a series of lectures given at the Kingston Liturgy Conference in Kingston, Ontario. The fourth on Christology, reconciliation and the required "consciousness for" ministry was sponsored by the Spiritual Renewal Center and the Religious Education Office in Syracuse, N.Y. The last, which deals with the question of Gnosticism and the role of women in esoteric Christianity, was part of the Conant Lecture series on Women in Church History at Bexley Hall in Rochester, N.Y. It was the only one prepared for a seminary audience, which included many women preparing for ministry in the Episcopal Church. The last lecture deals with the claims that esoteric Christianity preserved the place women had held in the Pauline mission after the orthodox community had adopted hierarchical forms of ministry that excluded women from participation. All three groups more than made up for the toil involved in shoving aside some of my personal plans for research, writing and even vacation during the past six months in order to work on this project.

Notes

1. See J. B. Metz, *The Emergent Church* (New York: Crossroad, 1981), 44–47. Metz sees "basic communities" as bearers of an anthropological revolution away from individualism and domination rooted in eucharistic symbolism and fundamental to the coming renewal of the whole Church.

2. See E. Schillebeeckx, *Ministry: Leadership in the Community of Jesus Christ* (New York: Crossroad, 1981), 96–98. Also see the discussion of New Testament evidence and the question of women's ordination by the Catholic Biblical Association Task Force on the Role of

Women in Early Christianity, "Women and Priestly Ministry: The New Testament Evidence," *Catholic Biblical Quarterly* 41 (1979), 608–13.

3. Metz, *op. cit.,* 82–93.

4. C. Davis, *Theology and Political Society* (Cambridge: Cambridge University, 1980), 74, insists on the necessity of consensus developed out of unrestrained dialogue for any social or political action undertaken by the Church. The same need for dialogue and consensus applies to other areas of Church life as well.

5. E. Braxton, *The Wisdom Community* (New York: Paulist, 1980).

6. See J. Schütz, *Paul and the Anatomy of Apostolic Authority* (Cambridge: Cambridge University, 1975), 7.

7. Schütz, *op. cit.,* ix–21. Schütz notes that the discussion is complicated by the confusion of power, authority and legitimacy.

8. See Schillebeeckx, *op. cit.,* 103f.

9. Schütz, *op. cit.,* 7, 31. Schütz notes that the usual understanding of "Church unity" is strained by the Pauline view of apostleship. Paul uses the image of "body" to bridge the gap between the individualized charismata and the goal of the Spirit's activity in the common life of Christians. The same priority of service binds both the apostle and any Christian, *op. cit.,* 255–59.

Chapter One

DISCIPLESHIP AND EVANGELIZATION

Introduction

Much of the material in the New Testament which describes the life of the disciple is formulated in sayings that applied to the life of the disciple-preacher. The sayings about abandoning all to follow Jesus reflect a life of itinerant radicalism of Christians who wandered from place to place healing and preaching the message of the kingdom. Matthew shows that later Christians applied the language of following Jesus to themselves even though the community was no longer composed of such wandering charismatics. Its members appear to have been settled, well-off Christians, not people living on the edges of society. Some members of the community may have continued to apply the sayings more literally to the life of discipleship. For others, by the time Matthew writes (80–90 C.E.), the logia about abandoning all for Jesus set forth the nature of discipleship, a singleminded devotion to Jesus. Such exhortations still had an important echo in the life of Christians, since they appear to have been subject to social harassment from both Jews and Gentiles (Mt 5:10–12, 44; 24:9).[1] Thus, these sayings provide a glimpse of one form of radical discipleship which became an ethical pattern of discipleship even for those who no longer felt called to abandon home, family and ethical convention literally.

The Matthean logia belong to the region of Syria and Palestine. They reflect the shifting fortunes of a community which can look directly back to Jesus and his disciples preaching among the Galilean villages even though members of that community no longer appear to be villagers themselves.[2] The Pauline letters provide glimpses of evangelism and discipleship in quite a different context, the cities of Asia Minor and Greece. Once again, Paul connects his model for discipleship, the lowliness and weakness of the crucified, with the life of his communities. They are to imitate him as he imitates Christ (e.g., 1 Cor 4:16).[3] This insistence that the apostle's weakness shows forth the power of God working in the Gospel was not simply a matter of speculation. Paul must establish this vision of apostleship and Christian life against competing visions which seek to ground their claims in the more direct manifestations of power and glory by the messengers of the Gospel and in the lives of Christians.[4] Recent sociological study of the Pauline churches has sought to understand these conflicts in terms of the social structure of Christians in the Hellenistic cities. They are not the impoverished masses but well-off artisans and the like who bring their own preconceptions of social hierarchy and their own struggle for superiority over their neighbors into the Christian community.[5] In addition to studies of social relationships in ancient cities, new studies of the spread of other religious cults have changed our understanding of religious associations in the cities of the ancient world. Mass conversions to Eastern cults as the remedy for social or psychological disorientation do not seem to have been common in this world and should not be hypothesized for the spread of Christianity.[6] The close-knit world of the ancient city and its trade associations make the behavior of individuals, which was always under public scrutiny,[7] one of the key elements of concern for the Christian community. We must recognize that a traditional, close-knit society does not embrace change with the enthusiasm of the twentieth-century Westerner. All the pressures and conventions of such a society go into maintaining what is traditional. Consequently, religious change in this society is better accounted for as the reorchestration of the traditional patterns than as their radical overthrow due to some outside influence.[8]

The "pullulation of beliefs"[9] in the ancient city has its foundations in the diverse origins of the populace. Christians were constantly on the defensive for having deserted their ancestral home, Judaism.[10] They had to give arguments that might validate such an apparent impiety and did so by proclaiming the superiority of "reason" to "superstition" or asserting their own claims to be the legitimate heirs of that tradition.[11] Such a situation could almost guarantee that conversion would be a fragile, shifting phenomenon. Paul must insist that unless it takes root in the ethical lives of the Corinthian converts, they will be as liable to judgment as those who remain unconverted.[12] 1 Thessalonians shows us that Paul sought to ground these concerns in the lives of his converts by addressing them in the paraenetic style common to the Cynic-Stoic moral philosophers of the first century.[13] The Pauline mission shows us the complex interaction of evangelization, discipleship and the traditional social and religious structures of the first century.

Evangelization Today: Catholicity, Critique and Dialogue

Before we return to the patterns of evangelization and discipleship in the first century, we should take a brief look at the problems of evangelization today. We do not suppose that our contemporary concerns are directly reflected in the first-century models. Not only do we live in a quite different social and political situation, but we also confront the question of evangelization as one of cultural pluralism. Our first-century models, by contrast, spoke to those with whom they shared a cultural base and many common presuppositions about ethics and religion. The first-century apostle addressing "the pagans" addresses those with whom he (or she) shares a common social life, a common trade, common patterns of dress, perhaps common friends or family relationships, a common city. Even the missionary in a strange city would have to find hospitality and therefore a partial "belonging" in the community before beginning to preach. Whatever hostility may follow, acceptance is the pre-condition for any entry into such a society. This pre-condition touches on one of the raw nerves of modern evangelization. Christian missions were too often outposts of colonialism. The paternalism and implicit cultural domination that accompanied those missionary efforts has been angrily rejected in the third world.[14]

Whatever the failures of the past, Christians cannot abandon mission. The catholicity of Christianity rests in its conviction that God's expression of salvation in Jesus is for all humans, not for a particular group or culture. That conviction has been rooted in Christianity since the sending of Jesus was first perceived as directed toward "the nations" and not simply the Jews.[15] We have seen that this impulse forced Christianity to become different from other religious movements, since it had to leave the Jewish fold and suffer the consequent charge of impiety toward its tradition. Today, theologians argue that just as Judaism and the philosophic traditions of the Graeco-Roman world provided the means for Christians to articulate their faith, so other cultures and religious traditions may come to provide new foundations for the discovery of Christ. Such a discovery is not possible until there has been a genuine dialogue with the cultures and traditions in question.[16] Such dialogue does not mean that Christian forms appropriate to those cultures will adopt every religious and social presupposition in them any more than Christians continued all the cultural patterns of the ancient world. However, it does require a certain disentanglement of Christianity from the cultural presuppositions of Western technological society. This disentanglement may work to the benefit of Christians everywhere if it calls the prevalent tendencies to self-assertive domination into question and reminds Christians of the biblical obligations toward the larger community.[17]

Although we have little experience of what such cross-cultural dialogue will lead to, it rests on some theological foundations which many theologians would consider central to Christianity. First, it assumes that the God we have come to know in Jesus Christ wills the salvation of all of humanity. This saving will is made effective through God's Spirit operating in all the great religious traditions.[18] Second, it assumes that humanity has a natural knowledge of and quest for God that has not been destroyed by sin. All humans know something about salvation. Third, it runs counter to the separatist tendencies of much religious fundamentalism. A genuinely catholic Christianity will not isolate itself in a ghetto of "the converted." Instead, it will join all those who seek to solve the genuine human problems of salvation that confront us.[19] Liberation theologians approach the problem of mission from the perspective of these human concerns. They argue that the love command and the identification of Jesus with the poor and outcast summon Christians to engage themselves in the struggle for justice and freedom. At the same time, they recognize that Christians are concerned about these questions because they know that the oppressed are the object of God's concern. They are not to become the bearers of a particular political project or social ideology. The Gospel warns us that no plan of social or political engineering can bring about the reordering of the human heart which is the foundation of conversion.[20] The Christian seeks reconciliation and genuine community, not the exaltation of one group over another.[21]

Christians today, then, recognize a new phase in the mission effort. The very nature of the Church binds it to seek the salvation of all humans. It cannot retreat into a limited ghetto. At the same time, the past history of colonialism requires a new sensitivity to cultural pluralism. The pre-condition of cultural dialogue and acceptance is more pressing than ever. For some theologians, such dialogue is the primary focus of the mission effort. For others, the pressing human concerns for freedom from poverty and oppression become the central concerns which unite Christians with others. They find the Gospel a word addressed to challenge all forms of human domination. Such a message can only be credible if uttered by those who show themselves willing to shoulder the burden of the struggle for liberation in the socio-political realm. The liberation approach often appeals to the ethic of itinerant radicalism, of discipleship as willing identification with the lowly of society. The dialogue approach, on the other hand, comes closer to the evangelism of the Pauline communities.

The Wandering Charismatic: Discipleship and Social Detachment

The ethic of discipleship in early Christian communities provided the impetus to continue the process initiated in conversion. Jesus and his disciples provided the earliest models for discipleship as they wandered from village to village in Galilee. Such disciples are radically detached from all the norms and traditions of the rural, village society. After Jesus' death, some Christians continued this pattern of itinerant healing and preaching. Collections of Jesus' sayings provided the basis for their way of life. The initial impetus for such preaching was probably to continue Jesus' summons to Israel to repent in light of the presence of the rule of God. Mt 10:5 preserves a saying limiting the mission to Israel. However, Christians soon realized that the traditional expectation of a renewal of Israel that would lead the other peoples of the world to acknowledge her God was not the form that events were taking. Israel continued to reject the Messiah while Gentiles were coming to acknowledge God and believe in salvation through Jesus.[22] All of the evangelists presume that Gentiles as well as Jews are called to belong to the kingdom.

The mission charge in Lk 10:1–12 and its parallels in Mt's longer set of instructions to missionaries appear to derive from a common collection of Jesus' sayings (=Q). The Q community combined motifs from the wisdom tradition with those of prophetic preaching. Its missionaries announced the impending return of Jesus as judge. They also experienced hostility and persecution as a result of their missionary efforts.[23] Here is Lk's version with its Matthean parallels:

Lk 10:2–12:	*Mt 9:37f; 10:16,9,10a, 11–13,10b,7f,14f:*
And he said to them,	Then he said to his disciples,
"The harvest is plentiful but the laborers are few; pray therefore the lord of the harvest to send out laborers into his harvest.	"The harvest is plentiful but the laborers are few; pray therefore the lord of the harvest to send out laborers into his harvest.
Go your way and behold, I send you out as lambs in the midst of wolves.	Lo, I send you out as sheep in the midst of wolves; so be wise as serpents and innocent as doves.
Carry no purse,	Take no gold, nor silver, nor copper in your belts,
no bag,	no bag for your journey, nor two tunics,
no sandals;	nor sandals, nor a staff. . . .
and salute no one on the road.	

And whatever town or village you enter,
find out who is worthy in it, and stay
with him until you depart.

Whatever house you enter, first
say, "Peace be to this house,"
And if a son of peace is there,
your peace shall rest upon him,
but if not, it shall return to you.
And remain in the same house,
eating and drinking what they
provide,
for the laborer deserves his
    wages;
do not go from house to house.
Whenever you enter a town and
    they
receive you, eat what is set
before you;
heal the sick in it and say
    to them,
"The kingdom of God has
    come near you."

As you enter the house, salute it. And
if the house is worthy let your peace
come upon it; but if it is not worthy,
let your peace return to you.

. . . for the laborer deserves his food.

And preach as you go saying, "The
    kingdom
of heaven is at hand." Heal the sick,
raise the dead, cleanse lepers, cast out
demons.
You received without pay, give without
    pay.

But whenever you enter
    a town and
they do not receive you, go into
its streets and say,
"Even the dust of your town that
clings to our feet, we wipe off
against you;
nevertheless know this, that the
kingdom of God has come near."
I tell you, it shall be more
tolerable on that day
for Sodom
than for that town.

And if anyone will not receive you,
or listen to your words,
shake off the dust
from your feet as you leave that
house or town.

Truly, I say to you, it shall be more
tolerable on the day of judgment
for the land of Sodom and Gomorrah
than for that town.

Both evangelists have edited the sayings somewhat. Mt's list
of healings summarizes the healings that Jesus has just performed. He makes it clear that the disciples are continuing the

messianic work of Jesus.[24] Lk 10:9 represents the association of healing and preaching by the wandering missionaries that leads scholars to speak of them as charismatic. The order to heal and then preach provides an important foundation for the proclamation of the kingdom. The prophetic preaching of these missionaries interprets the experience of healing witnessed by the audience. This pattern fits the picture of conversion in antiquity generally.[25] Theologians also point to the significance of this pattern as a general practice. The Gospel is not to be preached in a vacuum. It only makes sense when announced as the interpretation of a new experience of salvation.[26]

One of the fundamental rules implied in these sayings is that the missionary must be radically dependent upon his reception. He may not carry provisions from place to place. He must accept whatever hospitality he is given. And, in the Matthean case, which envisages the wealthier communities of a town rather than a village, he must not move from the place in which he initially settles. (This avoids the problem of favoring a wealthier patron who may wish to offer the missionary hospitality later.) Sayings of the Lord about the reception and wages of missionaries were widely circulated in early Christianity. Paul refers to them when he explains why he does not exercise his apostolic right to claim support from the community in which he is preaching (1 Cor 9:3–18). His opponents may have taken his decision to work rather than exercise this right as an indication that Paul did not have apostolic authority.[27] Paul pursues the debate in terms derived from the debate over proper support by the wandering Cynic-Stoic philosophers. Some condemned those who accepted support from a wealthy patron rather than live in absolute poverty; such persons exchange the freedom of the "wise person" for slavery. Paul adopts the freedom/slavery language to his commission (not free) to preach the Gospel (which he does freely and not for wages).[28] This argument shows that Paul is in some difficulty, since his practice does not conform to that of others. Further, 1 Cor 9:14 alludes to the type of tradition in the Q passage. But Paul's application to his own case is the opposite of that intended. The Q tradition instructs the missionary not to demand wages but to be content with whatever hospitality is received. The saying that Paul quotes implies that the missionary is not to provide for himself but is to be devoted full-time to the Gospel. Yet, Paul insists that these commandments are not obligations laid on all missionaries but rights which they are free to exercise or not. (Indeed, Paul did receive aid from other communities.) Paul insists that his practice avoids placing a hindrance in the way of the Gospel. This example shows a characteristic approach to the sayings of Jesus. Paul understands them as guidelines which must be critically evaluated in the particular circumstances to which they are to be applied.[29] In other discussions of the same issue, Paul comments that he does not wish to "burden" anyone (1 Thess 2:7; 2 Cor 11:9). The difference between his situation and that of the wandering charismatic envisaged by the original sayings may have been partially due to the length of time that he stayed in a city. Hospitality for a few days while healing and preaching in a village or town is quite different from staying in a city for long periods of time. Paul's trade makes it possible for him to remain without becoming a burden, though his expenses were also covered by gifts from members of other communities (2 Cor 11:8; Phil 4:15–18).[30] Thus, Paul is sure that such instructions must be understood in light of the larger responsibility that the apostle has for the Gospel.

The life of the wandering charismatic demanded a decisive break with the ethos of village and family life. The Markan stories of Jesus' family and fellow townspeople point to the kind of rejection and hostility which must have been common (Mk 3:21; 6:4). We have already seen that the wandering disciple had abandoned possessions and is radically dependent upon others. In the ethos of village life, the break with ("hatred of") family (Lk 14:26–27; Mt 10:37–38) stands as a clear example of the demand of the Gospel. The ties of both family and property run deep in a village culture. Consequently, Q contains several sayings which demand the most radical break with the family: the sword, not peace (Lk 12:53/Mt 10:35); not even the duty to bury a parent overrides the call to discipleship (Lk 9:59/Mt 8:21).[31] The most radical form of the break with family is reflected in the saying about those who are "eunuchs for the sake of the kingdom" (Mt 19:10f). This saying does not appear to have been as widely circulated as many of the others. Yet Paul, too, has his version of that injunction, "Be as I am" (1 Cor 7:8, 32–35, 39–40). He does not appeal to Jesus but to his own state and to the shortness and distress of the time before the judgment in making his recommendation. The cases which follow show that he will not make such advice a rule. Each individual must decide his or her case as the Spirit directs. The sayings about anxiety acknowledge the difficulties inherent in the life of the disciple (Mt 6:25–34/Lk 12:22–31; Mt 10:26–31/Lk 12:2–7).[32]

We have seen that the disciples are not to fight rejection. The sayings on love of enemies also have a concrete application to the situation faced by such missionaries. Love and non-retaliation leave open the possibility that the persecutor may be converted.[33] Once again, Paul has applied this tradition to his own experience as an apostle. It characterizes the apostle's behavior in the face of hostility (1 Cor 4:12b–13). the Corinthians are to learn from this example more than the "love of enemies." They are to learn the "power through weakness" by which the apostle represents Christ.[34] A related pattern appears in the various logia which enjoin the disciple to take up the cross (Mt 16:24; Mk 8:34; Lk 9:23). Thus, Paul has not invented this pattern of discipleship. He has given it a concrete expression in the context of his own apostolic experience. We have seen that the Matthean community takes the discipleship sayings as indicative of the spirit which should animate all members of the community. All must testify in the face of hostility from friends, neighbors, and family. Consequently, the sayings about fear, confession, and bearing the cross have meaning for all, not just the missionaries.[35] Paul's extension of the apostolic example to members of his communities presents a similar pattern. At the same time, Paul also suggests other principles for application of the sayings on discipleship to the life of the traveling apostle. The sayings establish "rights," not obligations. They suggest appropriate actions and ways of life; they do not legislate them. The appropriate application of these sayings must be discerned for the particular context, even for the particular apostle. What the Spirit dictates cannot be established a priori. If Paul felt the necessity of such context-determined interpretation in his mission, how much the more so today. Anyone who would insist upon a normative application of these sayings, whether in support of ecclesial traditions or in defense of a single ideology of liberation, can hardly stand on the same ground set by the apostle. One must defend the adequacy of a given application of the traditions of charismatic discipleship to proclaiming the Gospel in a concrete situation. Whether one approves of his conclusions or not, Paul shows that such arguments are a possible and legitimate part of the apostolic task.

Community and Conversion in the Graeco-Roman Cities

Neither the wandering charismatics of Syria and Palestine nor the wandering apostle, perhaps modeled on the Cynic preacher, could create a new form of religious community.

Both depend upon "marginality," on standing over against the values, conventions and concerns of most humans.[36] Paul is constantly concerned for the welfare of the communities he has left behind. His letters seek to direct their affairs when he is absent as does the group of close associates who accompany Pau.[37] He may have been tied to the Philippian community in a more formal arrangement, the legal *koinonia.* They constituted an association for the preaching of the Gospel. Such associations assigned different tasks to the parties to the agreement. Paul has received financial assistance from the Philippians as their part in this arrangement. Phil 4:10–20 uses the legal language expected of one partner acknowledging receipt of funds in payment of the expenses occurred while carrying out the work of the association. Paul may have had such relationships with other groups or individuals, though it does not form a fixed pattern in all of his relationships.[38] The turmoil in the Corinthian community would have made it impossible for them to enter into such a relationship with the apostle.[39] Paul's use of *societas,* a term for the open, non-deceitful, equal relationships between partners, indicates that it represents the ideal relationship between the apostle and the community. They are now equal partners in the Gospel.[40]

The Philippian community appears to have supported other missionaries as well. Paul mentions several who have worked with him for the Gospel, including two women. The exhortation that they "be of one mind in the Lord" represents the technical language of a *societas.* All members must continue to agree on and devote themselves to the purposes for which the original association was formed. Paul expects these two women to work together for the original purpose of the association.[41] Paul also uses expressions related to this one to ground the relationships within the community. "Having the same mind" implies love, peace, humility and concern for the interests of others. It rules out selfishness, conceit and concern only for one's own interests (Phil 2:1–5). The Christ hymn of Phil 2:6–11 grounds "the mind" of this *societas* not in the legal requirements for honesty and agreement among members of an association but in the example of Christ himself.[42] The language of this hymn recalls many of the honorific phrases of Roman social relations. Whatever the original background of the hymn, within the language context of Philippians it suggests what would seem to be socially unthinkable—that someone at the top of the steep social pyramid, someone "like God," would willingly descend to take on the form of slavery. In a world marked at all levels with the struggle for honorific titles, for superiority over one's fellows and even for the right to insult someone of lower status, the paradox of this hymn would not be lost.[43] Paul is concerned lest his absence permit the same attitudes to destroy the *koinonia* of the Philippians. His concerns may have been intensified by the legal convention that the absence of a partner to the *societas*—or the death of a partner—dissolved the association. Its members could form another association as they chose. Paul also uses a legal remedy to counter this possiblity. He reminds the Philippians that he intends to send his duly constituted representative, Timothy (Phil 2:19).[44] When we come to the Corinthian situation in the next chapter, we will see how easily the competitiveness and hierarchical concerns of ancient society can even use "spiritual gifts" to destroy the very heart of a Christian community.

One of the important sources of growth and support for religious movements was the system of patronage. Pagan religious activity with its temples, halls, banquets and festivals was expensive. Trade guilds might also raise funds for such expenses, but the usual route was to find the support of a wealthy patron. Such persons in effect controlled the religious options available in a community. Wealthy women might also be the source of funds. Occasional inscriptions suggest that some even headed associations dedicated to a particular god. Members of a single clan or household might control the offices in such an association. Further, there was no expectation that different cult associations devoted to the same deity had anything like a uniform cult.[45] Though the physical outlay of the Christian cult might be considerably less expensive, nevertheless Christians, too, avail themselves of wealthy patrons. The house churches in which the local communities met appear to be sponsored by wealthy heads of households. Several women appear in such roles in the Pauline letters, including Lydia at Philippi (Acts 16:40). Rom 16:1–2 is a brief note of recommendation for another such woman, Phoebe, deacon of the church at Chenchreae. Paul is instructing the recipients to aid her with her affairs. It may be that she has even undertaken the journey on behalf of the community—a pattern well-attested for male patrons. Careful studies of the spread of pagan cults that were popular during this period shows them to have been spread by members of families and households who moved from place to place, not by appeal to masses of new converts. The growth of Eastern cults in Italy is due to the influx of non-Italians. Similar mobility characterizes those who appear in the Pauline letters as leaders of house churches. Consequently, such relationships were not only fundamental to the structuring of local communities, they were also a major element in the spread of Christianity.[46] However, conflicts could also develop between the leaders of different household churches.

Phil 3:1—4:1 highlights another sociological facet of the early communities which created some tension within them. The first place Paul would begin his preaching was among those who were "God fearers," persons attracted by the monotheistic and ethical ideals of Judaism who had not yet become full proselytes. Some scholars suggest that these persons were of higher social standing than proselytes. Christianity may have appeared to offer the advantages of Judaism without the objectionable practices of circumcision and rituals associated with kosher food which would have made it impossible for such a person to continue normal social relationships with friends and family.[47] The negative picture of the Jew as one who "hated humanity," practiced circumcision, engaged in poor, lower class occupations, and scorned outsiders is widely drawn in antiquity. It forms the basis of their portrayal in comedy. They are accused of turning proselytes against their families.[48] Within the Jewish community, proselytes remained "second class" citizens. Even children who converted with their fathers could not inherit property, since they had been born "pagans."[49] It is easy to see that Christianity might attract such people. It is also easy to see that the outbreaks of violence between the Jewish population and Christian missionaries attested both in Acts and in the edict banning Jews from Rome for rioting at the name of *Chrestus* under Claudius could easily be provoked when the Christian preachers won these influential sympathizers away from the local synagogue communities. This segment of a letter between Paul and the Philippians castigates those who would destroy the *koinonia* of the Philippian community by introducing Judaizing customs. Paul's severe conflict over a similar issue in Galatia shows the appeal that those who preached a more Jewish form of Christianity had for Gentile converts. Were they to gain a foothold in Philippi they would destroy one of the central themes of the Pauline Gospel: through Christ Gentiles can share in the blessings of the God of Israel without passing through the law, without adopting Jewish customs.[50]

Christians were also aware that their mode of life was an essential factor in evangelization. The "household codes" and tables of duties in many early Christian writings make it clear that Christians expect their superior standard of behavior to erase any suspicions a tradition-oriented society might have of the new movement.[51] 1 Pet orients the whole ethic of the community toward the task of erasing cause for hostility and bringing non-Christians to glorify God.[52] This stance within the larger society forms the essence of the community's claim to represent the "new Israel." The combination of a highly mobile group of members and the conviction that Christianity represents the messianic people of God helped foster an important difference between Christians and friends who might support other cults. The Christians saw themselves as members of a universal movement. Consequently, differences over teaching and practice between different Christian groups were taken more seriously than they were in the pagan cults which had no concept of or process for such unity. The Johannine traditions gave a theological reading to the testimony of the local community. All Christians were to share in the "sending of Jesus" to the world.[53]

Summary

The New Testament conviction that God's salvation is "for all" led to a concern for evangelization and for universality that is unusual among the religious movements of its time. Inevitably, that concern could not be formalized in a single pattern of discipleship. The sayings of Jesus which sponsored the efforts of wandering, charismatic preachers in the villages of Galilee and Syria themselves gave rise to other patterns of life. For Christians settled in the towns of the Matthean Church they present the fundamental change of heart required of all disciples. For the traveling apostles in the Hellenistic cities, they indicate "rights" which pattern the life of the missionary. However, Paul insists that such "rights" do not have the force of laws. They must be applied to the particular individuals and circumstances in which the apostle works. We also see that the complexities of social critique and social integration are handled in different ways by early Christians. The more radical sayings about discipleship assume that some Christians will move out of the conventions of their society. The communities of the Hellenistic cities, on the other hand, are more closely tied to the social patterns accepted in the first century. However, they cannot permit the disruptive elements of hierarchy, ambition and self-exaltation to erode the foundations of a community that is to be based on "the same mind," the example of Christ, who is exalted precisely because he sets aside common patterns of behavior. Finally, the perception of universality which underlies the Christian commitment to evangelization continues to be the goal of the community, which is not perfectly realized. Divisions between Christians, fractured *koinonia*, and the disputes over Judaizing all show a Church on the way, discovering in the process the sort of people over which Christ is Lord. Our own discussions of mission must continue the process of discovery.

Notes

1. See J. D. Kingsbury, "The Very *Akolouthein* ("To Follow") as an Index of Matthew's View of his Community," *Journal of Biblical Literature* 97 (1978), 56–73. Kingsbury describes the Matthean community as in a period of ethical transition. Unlike Lk 22:35f, Mt does not revise the ethic of itinerant radicalism. That ethic still has important ties to the life of the community. It guides those who continue to be traveling missionaries, and it dictates the proper response to the community's experiences of persecution.

2. Kingsbury, *op cit.*, 66–71. Mt's revisions make the domiciled and urban character of his community clear.

3. See Schütz, *op. cit.*, 226–32.

4. See Schütz's discussion of the Corinthian situation, *op. cit.*, 187–203. Schütz points out that both here and in Galatians Paul sidesteps the issue of competing claims to authority.

5. For a general discussion of class, social stratification and ur-

ban guilds see R. MacMullen, *Roman Social Relations. 50 B.C. to A.D. 248* (New Haven: Yale, 1974), 57–120. For a general survey of sociological approaches to the New Testament see R. Scroggs, "The Sociological Interpretation of the New Testament: The Present State of Research," *New Testament Studies* 26 (1980), 164–79.

6. See R. MacMullen, *Paganism in the Roman Empire* (New Haven: Yale, 1981), 94–112. MacMullen points out that all testimonies show visible displays of divine power and effective oratory to be important factors in gaining attention. Pagan cults might also use inscriptions, cult buildings and festivals to draw crowds.

7. P. Brown, *The Making of Late Antiquity* (Cambridge: Harvard, 1978), 3–5. Brown points out that this is a face-to-face society in which there is little privacy. One's whole life is subject to social control. The problems which confront persons in such societies are claustrophobia and tensions like anger and envy, not loneliness or rootlessness.

8. Brown, *op. cit.*, 7–11.

9. MacMullen, *Paganism*, 1.

10. *Ibid.*, 2f.

11. See the discussion of the answers to such objections developed by the apologists in R. Wilken, "The Christians as the Romans (and Greeks) Saw Them," *Jewish and Christian Self-Definition*, ed. E. P. Sanders (Philadelphia: Fortress, 1980), 102–23.

12. For example, 1 Cor 8—10. See J. Murphy-O'Connor, *1 Corinthians* (Wilmington: Michael Glazier, 1979), 76–103.

13. See A. Malherbe, *Social Aspects of Early Christianity* (Baton Rouge: Louisiana State, 1977), 22–27.

14. See H. Dapper, *Mission-Glaubensinterpretations-Glaubensrealisation. Ein Beitrag zur ökumenischen Missiontheologie* (Frankfort: Peter Lang, 1979), 19–88.

15. Dapper, *op. cit.*, 70–75. Dapper emphasizes the Johannine images of the sending of the Son by the Father as the grounding of the sending of the disciples to the world.

16. J. R. W. Stott, "The Biblical Basis of Evangelism," *Mission Trends No. 2: Evangelization*, eds. G. Anderson and T. Stransky (New York: Paulist; Grand Rapids: Eerdmans, 1975), 13–15.

17. Metz, *op. cit.*, 42–47.

18. See the theological discussion by K. Rahner, "Jesus Christ in the Non-Christian Religions," *Theological Investigations XVII* (New York: Crossroad, 1981), 39–50.

19. Dapper, *op. cit.*, 131–33, 164–68.

20. *Ibid.*, 89–130.

21. *Ibid.*, 172–79.

22. Mk 13:10 reflects the older view. See the treatment of this topic in S. G. Wilson, *The Gentiles and the Gentile Mission in Luke-Acts* (Cambridge: Cambridge University, 1973), 3–47.

23. See R. Edwards, *A Theology of Q. Eschatology, Prophecy and Wisdom* (Philadelphia: Fortress, 1976), 102–104.

24. See H. Held, in G. Bornkamm, G. Barth and H. J. Held, *Tradition and Interpretation in Matthew* (Philadelphia: Westminster, 1963), 250–52.

25. MacMullen, *Paganism*, 96.

26. Dapper, *op. cit.*, 179f.

27. Schütz, *op. cit.*, 235.

28. R. Hock, *The Social Context of Paul's Ministry. Tentmaking and Apostleship* (Philadelphia: Fortress, 1980), 50–62.

29. Murphy-O'Connor, *1 Corinthians*, 86–89.

30. Hock, *op. cit.*, 29–31.

31. Edwards, *op. cit.*, 135.

32. G. Theissen, *Sociology of Early Palestinian Christianity* (Philadelphia: Fortress, 1978), 8–16.

33. L. Schottroff, "Non-Violence and the Love of Enemies," *Essays on the Love Command*, ed. R. Fuller (Philadelphia: Fortress, 1978), 9–39.

34. Schütz, *op. cit.*, 229.

35. Barth, *Tradition and Interpretation*, 99–101.

36. Theissen, *op. cit.*, 15.

37. Malherbe, *op. cit.*, 48.

38. P. Sampley, *Pauline Partnership in Christ. Christian Community and Commitment in Light of Roman Law* (Philadelphia: Fortress, 1980), 51–102. Sampley suggests that since "giving the right hand" is a formal part of such contractual associations, Gal 2:9 implies that Paul and the Jerusalem apostles had entered into such an agreement: pp. 27–36.

39. Sampley, *op. cit.*, 86f.

40. *Ibid.*, 61f. This special relationship also appears in the greeting of the letter. Here, in Phlm (which uses *koinonia* language of Paul's relationship with Philemon) and in 1 Thess we find that Paul does not assert his authority as apostle.

41. Phil 4:2–3. Sampley, *op. cit.*, 68f.

42. Ibid., 62–68.

43. On titles, honors and planned social insults, see MacMullen, *Social Relations,* 104–120.

44. Sampley, *op. cit.,* 87–91.

45. MacMullen, *Paganism,* 106–112.

46. On the growth of pagan cults through population migration, see MacMullen, *Paganism,* 114–17. On the house church structure of local Christian communities, see Malherbe, *op. cit.,* 60–74.

47. B. Holmberg, *Paul and Power* (Philadelphia: Fortress, 1980), 105f; Malherbe, *op. cit.,* 66–77.

48. See J. L. Daniel, "Anti-Semitism in the Hellenistic-Roman Period," *Journal of Biblical Literature* 98 (1979), 45–65.

49. J. Jeremias, *Jerusalem in the Time of Jesus* (Philadelphia: Fortress, 1969), 320–34.

50. See K. Stendahl, *Paul among Jews and Gentiles* (Philadelphia: Fortress, 1976), 1–40.

51. Malherbe, op. cit., 22.

52. J. Elliott, *The Elect and the Holy* (Leiden: E. J. Brill, 1966). See, for example, 1 Pet 2:4–10.

53. Dapper, *op. cit.,* 182.

Chapter Two

WORSHIP AND CHRISTIAN COMMUNITY IN PAUL

Introduction

The privatization of religion in our culture takes a heavy toll on our sense of community and liturgical celebration. We may have more empathy for the individualized religious ecstasy of the Corinthians than for Paul's message about worship and community. Both the time and sensibility for the celebration of communal realities and visions are hard to find in a world of "get ahead," ego-oriented men and women. Unless some real conversion in our mode of understanding ourselves takes place, all the assertions that the Church is the "people of God" and all the liturgical reforms in the world will not bring us to true celebration. We can only begin to confront the problem facing us when we recognize that the value and place of religion in our society is not appropriate to the biblical understanding of human community. Religion has become a consumer product along with any number of other "quick fix" cures marketed by the human potential movement. This "goods and services" approach says that if religious practice does not contribute to my happiness, success or ego-development, I should discard it in favor of something else that will.[1] M. Marty argues that the Bible cannot be called "wholistic" in

30

its portrayal of faith. It shows human attempts to create salvation and wholeness as failures. Its great heroes live out of hope. They are able to live with partial fulfillment.[2] The destruction of the bonds of human community by modern individuals also affects our theological reflection. Theology seeks to interpret to itself and to outsiders the life and language of a shared religious experience. Faced with the garbled utterances of private strivers, it loses the roots of its creative, symbol-making power.[3]

Liberation theologians have been the harshest critics of this decay in our communal life, since a genuine community of action must underlie the theological language of liberation. J. Metz points out that our liturgical imagery reinforces our sense of Church. While we have become somewhat sensitive to the liturgical expressions of the patriarchal Church, we have not attended to the dangers of "personal fulfillment" models, often adopted in the name of liturgical reform. Metz suggests that the very symbolism of the Eucharist carries a message about the human person which counters some of the unconscious presuppositions of our time. The Eucharist is about death. Yet twentieth-century Christians seem able to shut out the reality of death to such an extent that they can contemplate the brutal extermination of most of the race. The Eucharist is about human realities of loss, fear and mourning. It should not be turned into a "success-oriented" celebration. The Eucharist reminds us that the suffering of others are not their private tragedy. They are the tragedy of the whole community. Finally, the Eucharist celebrates the death of the Son of God. It does not celebrate self-fulfillment. It asks us to internalize a love which is the antithesis of the psycho-dynamics of power, of striving for success, of accumulating at the expense of others.[4]

Such a call for an anthropological renewal, for a move from the enlightenment of the individual to the betterment of the community and even to a sense of the priority of that community is fundamental to Paul's struggle with the Corinthians. The structures of a hierarchical and ambitious society had generated envy and divisive competition.[5] Spiritual gifts like speaking in tongues were apparently used by some as evidence of their superiority over others.[6] The rich, following a common pattern of social behavior, demonstrated their superiority to the poor by eating and drinking to excess at the Lord's supper while the poor went hungry.[7] The inferiors were expected to "take what they got" and be grateful. At Corinth, the offenders might have argued that they had done enough in providing the place and the basic essentials for the supper. If they had separate places and food for their friends, the others had no right to complain.[8] But however socially acceptable such behavior may have been, Paul insists that it cannot be allowed to corrupt the celebration of the Lord's supper. Just as he linked the *koinonia* among the Philippians with the image of Christ's death, so he recalls the tradition of the supper as the memory of that death. Such a memory can never be corrupted into an occasion for self-exaltation. The Corinthian example shows that even a wealth of religious experiences does not guarantee conversion. Paul insists that the outpouring of the Spirit in worship must be combined with a vision of the unity of that same Spirit working toward the building of the community. We do not yet belong to the "new creation" which the gifts of the Spirit promise. Love must root Christians in the realities of social life in this world.[9]

Thanksgiving, Foundation of Community

Paul has not invented the connection between liturgical commemoration of God's saving action and the formation of a community united by mutual obligation. This connection is fundamental to the biblical tradition. H. Guthrie has pointed to the organic connection between all stages in the biblical tradition and the liturgical celebration of God's salvation realized in the community. The fundamental response to God's action is thanksgiving (Heb. *todah;* Gk. *eucharistia*).[10] We need to orient our vision toward this perspective. Consciously or unconsciously, we tend to think of the Bible either as information about God or as rules for pleasing God. Such a perspective means that the fundamental response to the biblical message would be either teaching or legal interpretation. Of course, the biblical tradition does call forth both activities. However, we tend to make such activities central and lose sight of the biblical tradition as a community's act of thanksgiving for the salvation it has experienced.

Guthrie points out that we also need to recover the root meaning of "righteousness." We often assume that "righteousness" refers to people who please God by keeping commandments or to God as the one who rewards or punishes people in accord with their fidelity to those same commandments. The fundamental meaning of "righteousness" cannot be captured in such a legal model. "Righteousness" refers to God's gracious action in response to human need. The biblical narrative testifies to that action, to the effective power of God. It contains the promise that God is loving fidelity (*hesed*). God's actions in the future will be like those in the past. The biblical community would not exist if it were not for God's action calling it into being. It does not have some claim to existence apart from God on "natural," that is, racial, ethnic, geographical grounds.[11] We have seen that for the Christian community the call goes to "all" to be part of the community of salvation. As such, it implied the formation of a community that was not entirely like the other patterns of association in the Graeco-Roman world, since it did not fall into traditional social divisions, class distinctions or ethnic boundaries between Jew and Gentile. Paul centers the founding of this community in the cross, the death of Jesus encoded in the symbols of the eucharistic celebration. The liturgical act of thanksgiving for salvation, even for the very existence of the community, must always have priority over the law. Obedience to the law in the biblical tradition is also a response to the salvation found at the origins of the community. The law does not constitute or define the community. Those who lose the perspective of thanksgiving can turn the biblical tradition into information or into a type of wisdom which becomes the property of an elite, those who are able to interpret it.[12]

Paul's struggle with the Corinthians is to assert the priority of thanksgiving in response to God's saving action (the Gospel as "power") over wisdom. Thanksgiving obliges the community to see that it continues the salvation of God begun with the people of Israel, and still subject to the possibility of judgment as they had been (1 Cor 10:1–13). That same community is also the mediator through which the power of God is to become effective in the world.[13] Thus, Paul insists that actions which the Corinthians apparently thought morally neutral since their spiritual gifts continued,[14] like participating in feasts at pagan temples (1 Cor 10:14–22), may really bring condemnation. They destroy the community, the *koinonia* in Christ. Paul's difficulties in Corinth may have been increased by the dominance of the law in Jewish religious consciousness and the expectation that religious writings contain esoteric wisdom among some pagans. Elsewhere, Paul has had to face those who think that Christianity is to be revised interpretation of the law. In Corinth, he is confronted with those who value ecstatic illumination and divine wisdom. Paul insists that the community is not founded on either law or wisdom, a circle of elite interpreters. It is grounded in thanksgiving for the power of God now activated in human history through the death and resurrection of Christ.[15] The expression "Gospel" around which Paul orchestrates so much of his religious symbolism[16] reflects the prophetic promise of salvation in Is 52:7.[17] Just as the prophetic vision implied a real transformation of human life, the Gospel proclaims that the divine power for that transformation has been released in the world. From Paul's day to our own, Christians must continue to ask, "What are the consequences of this introduction of the Gospel into the history of humanity? What is the significance of this new gathering of the people of God based on the reconciliation brought about in the death of Jesus?"

Spiritual Gifts and the Power of the Gospel

The transforming power of the Spirit cannot be identified with ecstatic religious phenomena. Paul's difficulties with the Corinthians show that spiritual gifts like tongues and prophecy are not self-interpreting. The Corinthians presumed that these manifestations of divine power showed that their own transformation into a "new creation" was complete. They manifested their new status in disregard for social conventions and lack of concern for the impact of their behavior on others.[18] References to the link between the preaching of the Gospel and manifestations of the Spirit in Paul's letters make it clear that the initial proclamation of the Gospel was the occasion for an outpouring of the Spirit.[19] Spiritual gifts continued to be a regular part of the life of Christian communities (Gal 3:1–14; 1 Thess 1:4–6; 1 Cor 2:4–6). Gal 3:5 takes it for granted that the inaugural outpouring of the Spirit continues in the life of the community: "Does he who supplies the Spirit to you and works miracles among you do so by works of the law or by hearing with faith?"[20]

The gifts of the Spirit are being used by the Corinthians in such a way that the foundations of the community are undermined. Many of the problems associated with the spiritual gifts appear to stem from their combination with social patterns of power and prestige. Those who served as patrons of the community would expect its religious activities to contribute to their own glory. Privilege and community adulation were considered the due of those who shouldered the obligations of patronage. They expect their position at the head of the social hierarchy to be enhanced.[21] Normally, banquets would distinguish between guests of high and low social status by serving choice food and wine to those at the head table and worse food to those of lower status. Occasionally, we hear of a banquet at a religious festival being held without a head table. Such a celebration would emphasize the festal release from social restrictions.[22] The Corinthian celebration of the Lord's supper clearly followed the conventional patterns. The rich were getting drunk; the poor, going hungry. Paul castigates them for this deliberate humiliation of the poor:

> When you meet together, it is not the Lord's Supper that you eat. For, in eating, each one goes ahead with his own meal, and one is hungry and another is drunk. What! Do you not have houses to eat and drink in? Or do you despise the Church of God and humiliate those who have nothing? What shall I say to you? Shall I commend you in this? No, I will not. (1 Cor 11:20–22)

The competitiveness and self-exaltation of ancient society also influenced the Corinthian evaluation of other spiritual gifts. Those with the more spectacular gifts claimed superiority over those without them. Paul does not argue against this mixture of cultural assumptions, spiritual gifts and half-digested Christianity on the basis of a commitment to reverse all the values of society. He is often accused of an unduly reactionary concern for preserving social order when he advises slaves to "stay in your calling" (1 Cor 7:20–24).[23] Paul's argument against the Corinthian treatment of spiritual gifts is theological. The community as body of Christ is still bound to God's judgment. The invasion of social prejudice and deliberate humiliation of members of that community into the celebration of the Lord's supper destroys the very core of God's act of salvation.[24]

Paul never denies that the spiritual gifts of which the Corinthians are so proud come from God. He agrees that such gifts are a desirable part of Christian life.[25] However, these gifts can only be properly used if they are subject to two criteria. First, all gifts come from one Spirit and aim at the building up of the community, not at tearing it apart with division. Second, though Christians live out of such experiences of the Spirit, these experiences are not the fullness of the kindgom. They do not reflect the eschatological perfection to which God's saving activity will bring creation. Those who thought that they could eat any meat sold in the market, whether or not it had been offered to idols, were right in asserting that idols were nothing. However, they failed to realize that if their action causes someone else to lose faith, destroys a fellow Christian, then all the theological insight in the world cannot make that action right. The most important gift for building up the community is love. It acknowledges the problems created by the conscience of those for whom the idols are still "something." In so doing it acknowledges the fact that the community is not the kingdom. The community still lives in the old creation even with the new power of God which has broken into human experience. Paul uses the priority of love to stand all the other Corinthian values on end (1 Cor 12:31b—13:3).[26] The dramatic gifts which mean so much to the Corinthians are really perishable. They belong to this period of Christian life between the death of Christ and the parousia. Thus, they are really signs of the fact that Christians still live in a world of imperfection. Paul even applies this reservation to prophecy which knows the eschatological secrets, the mysteries of God's plan of salvation. The real sign of eschatological perfection in the community is love, which works toward building up the community.[27]

Building Up the Community as Ordo for Worship

Following the chapter on love, Paul returns to the problems of worship in Corinth. He stresses building up the community as the basis for regulation of the practice of prophetic speech.[28] Building up the community is closely tied to encouragement and exhortation (*parakalein*).[29] Both concepts originate in the Pauline mission. Exhortation is fundamental to apostolic preaching (1 Thess 2:11; Phil 2:1). God may be said to exhort through the apostle (2 Cor 5:10; Rom 12:1) or through Scripture (Rom 15:4f). However, exhortation is not limited to the apostle. Christians also serve one another through mutual exhortation (1 Thess 4:18; 5:11).[30] 1 Thessalonians is an exhortation letter which serves as a good example of the type of speech Paul has in mind when he refers to exhortation.[31] He instructs the Thessalonians to console one another with the prophetic word of the Lord about the righteous dead (1 Thess 4:18). The insight into the future embodied in this prophetic word is the ground for the hope which Christians have in the present. Thus, prophecy and exhortation belong together in speaking for building up the community.[32]

1 Cor 14:26 makes "building up" the community the fundamental criterion for any use of prophetic speech within the worship of the community. Of course, Paul presumes throughout that spiritual gifts are always under the control of the recipient. People can refrain from speaking in tongues if there is no interpreter. People can cease prophesying if someone else is inspired. Paul insists that the most important use of speech in the liturgical context is intelligible speech which edifies the

community. Such intelligible speech enables others to participate by affirming the message delivered:

> So with yourselves, since you are eager for manifesta-
> tions of the Spirit, strive to excel in building up the
> Church. Therefore, he who speaks in a tongue should
> pray for the power to interpret. For, if I pray in a
> tongue my spirit prays, but my mind is unfruitful.
> What am I to do? I will pray with the spirit and I will
> pray with the mind also. I will sing with the spirit
> and I will sing with the mind also. Otherwise, if you
> bless with the spirit, how can anyone in the position
> of an outsider say the "Amen" to your thanksgiving
> when he does not know what you are saying? For you
> may give thanks well enough, but the other person is
> not edified. I thank God that I speak in tongues more
> than you all; nevertheless, in the Church I would
> rather speak five words with my mind in order to in-
> struct others, than ten thousand words in a tongue.
> (1 Cor 14:12–19)

Contrary to what some of his contemporaries may have
thought, Paul will not grant that control of the mind by the
divine spirit is the highest manifestation of the spiritual life.
Such a gift has no function in the community-building work of
the Spirit. Paul implies that it does not even edify the person
possessed of such a gift. Instead, he argues that one should
seek to instruct others so that they can participate in affirming the thanksgiving that lies at the heart of Christian worship.[33]
    Paul continues the argument in an even more striking
vein. The heart of Christian liturgical speaking is not just directed to "insiders"; it is also directed toward the conversion
of outsiders, toward evangelization. Indeed, Paul understands
his apostolic mission as a commission given by God for "building up" (2 Cor 10:8; 13:10; 1 Cor 3:10–12; 1 Thess 5:11). Pro-

phetic speech builds up the community in the most fundamental sense when it brings the outsider to acknowledge God:

> Brethren, do not be children in your thinking; be babes in evil, but in thinking be mature. In the law, it is written: "By men of strange tongues and by the lips of foreigners will I speak to this people, and even then they will not listen to me, says the Lord." Thus, tongues are a sign not for believers but for unbelievers, while prophecy is not for unbelievers but for believers. If, therefore, the whole Church assembles and all speak in tongues, and outsiders or unbelievers enter, will they not say that you are mad? But if all prophesy, and an unbeliever or an outsider enters, he is convicted by all, he is called to account by all, the secrets of his heart are disclosed; and so, falling on his face, he will worship God and declare that God is really among you. (1 Cor 14:20–25)

Paul has reinterpreted the prophetic word directed to Israel as proof that tongues can only serve a negative function. They can only confirm people in their unbelief, since Christians will be taken to be another strange ecstatic cult. The real sign of God's presence in the community is the word which unmasks the secrets of the heart and leads to conversion.[34] The unbeliever coming to praise God alludes to the promise of Is 45:14, which he sees fulfilled in the Christian community: the nations come to praise the God of Israel and acknowledge God's presence.[35] Thus, Paul has set speaking within the community in the context of that salvation from God which has come to humanity in Christ. God seeks to bring others into that action of thanksgiving and praise.

Paul concludes the chapter with some rules that are to order worship. It appears that Paul did not have any specific person or persons to commission to take charge. Presumably the person in whose house the meeting was held would be responsible for seeing that proper order was observed.[36] The lack of any local leaders acknowledged by all may be responsible for the fact that Paul throws all of his personal authority and the custom of other churches behind these rules.[37] Yet the section of rules is distinguished from Paul's theological argument about the foundations of Christian worship. They are not derived from the theological categories of building up and exhortation. The closest analogies to these rules are rules of worship and conduct in other Jewish religious communities of the time. Paul has introduced them as a way of creating order in the Corinthian assemblies so that the primary goals outlined earlier in the chapter can be achieved.

"It Is Unseemly for a Woman to Speak in Public"

Most of the rules laid down in 1 Cor 14:26–40 have been properly understood by Christians for what they were—an ad hoc use of Jewish liturgical practices to meet a particular situation. However, the rule against women speaking in public has been treated differently. It has been enforced with varying degrees of severity in Christian Churches down to the present day (vv 33b–36). There is no warrant in the passage itself for such a distinction. Some interpreters have tried to suggest that these verses should be separated from their surroundings because they speak in the language of absolute prohibition. This language belongs more to the tradition of household ethical codes. Such preaching appears frequently later in the development of the Pauline communities. The prohibition of women teachers in 1 Tim 2:11–12 belongs in the context of such a household code. Christians adopted such codes to prove that they did not endanger social order. Since 1 Cor 11:5 presumes that women do pray and prophesy in the assembly, and since Paul does not prohibit their doing so but regulates the dress of both sexes, some exegetes even suggest that this section was a later interpolation into 1 Cor.[38] Whether or not such interpolation took place, the rule belongs to codes of accepted social behavior in the first century. It has no more claim to eternal validity than the other rules derived from common ethical codes. Since people would have generally agreed with the sentiment that it was unseemly for a woman to speak in public, one cannot presume that the rule says anything about how they should behave in a society which feels differently. We saw in the last chapter that Paul applies sayings of Jesus quite differently to his own situation than the way in which they were applied by others. He is not in principle opposed to adaptation of rules of this sort.

Although this passage reflects what people would have agreed was good behavior, there is evidence from Pompey and elsewhere that these conventions did not in fact control the lives of women. Women who had learned trades while slaves continued to pursue them. These trades are the same ones which formed the artisan base of the Corinthian community: wool trade, shopkeeper, artisan, building trade, money lender, butcher, fish-monger, dealer in luxury goods like purple dye. One woman owns a brick works, another a stone-cutting operation. Though women are said not to have been permitted to join guilds, Elimachia, the owner of the brickworks, is patron of the fullers' guild. She donated colonnades and porticoes to the city and built an imposing tomb for herself just as any male patron would have done. Women could join religious and burial guilds. Some even held offices in such guilds.[39] A few wealthy women even achieved the public acclaim of their community and the reward of a cult statue.[40]

Since women tend to be under-represented in inscriptions, their involvement in such activities may be presumed to have been more extensive than the surviving evidence. We have no indication that such activities caused any great alarm or comment. However, women were generally barred from legal and political assemblies. The sarcasm of verse 36 suggests that some serious breech of public decorum occurred at Corinth. We cannot say what that might have been. Christians had to avoid such behavior in order to show that charges or suspicions against them were groundless. Consequently, it is not surprising that they should be called to conform to the prevailing standards.

"Discerning the Body of Christ"

We have already seen that accepting prevailing standards did not involve following all social customs. Paul speaks out strongly against those accepted patterns of behavior which threatened to destroy the unity of the community. Just as he did in the section on worship and spiritual gifts, Paul separates the rules he introduces from his theological discussion of the significance of the "body of Christ." The rules to wait for one another and to eat at home if you are hungry come at the end of the chapter (1 Cor 11:33–34a). The Corinthians apparently held a meal during which the various abuses of separate food and divisive behavior took place. The sacramental enactment with the word over the bread and wine followed. Paul does not want to change the order of the meal, but he insists that the behavior toward each other during the meal is just as much a matter of salvation as the symbolic action with bread and wine.[41]

The formula which Paul quotes probably came from Antioch. Paul's interpretation of the formula begins in verse 26. He refers to the proclamation of the atoning death of the Lord which accompanied the rite. This ritual, he reminds the Corinthians, is also one of those spiritual gifts which applies to the present, "in between" existence of the Christian. They should acknowledge that fact, since the formula recalls the coming of the Lord to which Christians look. This consciousness of the incompleteness of present salvation was embodied in the Aramaic prayer to the Lord to come, "Maranatha" (1 Cor 16:22).[42] But because we live in a time of "unfinished" salvation, the Eucharist is not a guarantee of our perfection. It acknowledges both the salvation out of which the community is formed and the culmination of divine action that is expected when the Lord returns. But as long as we remain in this "in between" time we can still fail to attain that salvation. Paul warns the Corinthians that if they do not discern the body of the Lord, they may become guilty of that body and blood. This is a sober warning, indeed. It implies that they could place themselves in the same situation as those who had been responsible for the death of Christ (1 Cor 11:27).[43] This warning is similar to that issued in 1 Cor 8:11–13. There, the theologically correct Christian whose consumption of idol meat causes another Christian whose conscience is weak to lose faith actually sins against the Lord. Christ died for that weak Christian just as much as for the strong one. The behavior which has corrupted the Corinthian Lord's supper is described as failure to discern the body of Christ in the weak or poor members of the community who are being humiliated by the Corinthian behavior. Paul even warns that incidents of sickness and death in the community may not be neutral. They may be chastisements from God to warn the community that they must repent before they are caught up in the judgment which will come (vv 30–32). Paul does not mean that all sickness and death is a sign of sin. He is using a prophetic theme. God sends chastisements on his people so that they will repent. Paul may have needed such signs to counter the Corinthian view that the spiritual gifts present in their community were proof that God was with them.[44]

Summary

Thanksgiving for the salvation which brought the community into being should be the central focus of the liturgical life of the community. That thanksgiving should be expressed in speech which exhorts and therefore builds up the faith of those who belong to that community. That thanksgiving should also be expressed in prophetic speech which "convicts," which brings the outsider to share the same thanksgiving. Thus, thanksgiving also seeks to build up the community by bringing others to share that salvation. But such a community cannot persist in relationships that serve to honor and glorify some at the expense of others. It cannot persist in a privatized understanding of spiritual gifts, which fails to recognize that they are only given for the purpose of building up the community.

Paul attempts to teach the Corinthians to discern the body of Christ by recognizing that the relationships between Christians are modeled on the atoning death of Christ as salvation for all people. None of their relationships are exempt from this scrutiny. The body of Christ has no place for those relationships of power and privilege in which the weak, the poor and the slave are humiliated for the greater glory of the rich. For the rich Christian patron, this lesson must have been very difficult. It meant that the "psychological and personal rewards" which society had laboriously constructed to see that the rich assumed some responsibility for the welfare of the larger community had to be surrendered. Motivation for such a drastic change can only come from seeing the cross within the framework of thanksgiving. These Christians have no reason at all to expect the salvation that has called them into being. Yet, God has blessed them with an extraordinary outpouring of the Spirit. These gifts are not an occasion for self-exaltation, not an occasion for the heedless flaunting of all the conventions which hold human society together. They are the occasion for a life of discipleship which persists despite all obstacles in building up the body of Christ.

Notes

1. See M. Marty, *The Public Church* (New York: Crossroad, 1981), 25–34.

2. *Ibid.*, 29f.

3. *Ibid.*, 26.

4. Metz, *op. cit.*, 33–43.

5. Malherbe, *op. cit.*, 72–81.

6. Murphy-O'Connor, *1 Corinthians*, 117.

7. On deliberate insults at meals see MacMullen, *Social Relations*, 111.

8. Malherbe, *op. cit.*, 83f.

9. R. Horsley, "Consciousness and Freedom among the Corinthians," *Catholic Biblical Quarterly* 40 (1978), 586–88.

10. H. Guthrie, *Theology as Thanksgiving* (New York: Seabury, 1981).

11. Early Israel was a people of diverse tribal origins bound together by their entry into the covenant. The identification of Jews as an ethnic group is a post-exilic phenomenon; see G. Mendenhall, *The Tenth Generation* (Baltimore: Johns Hopkins, 1973), 14–20, 226.

12. Guthrie, *op. cit.*, 149–69.

13. *Ibid.*, 44–66.

14. On the Corinthian use of spiritual gifts to support their claims, see J. Murphy-O'Connor, "Food and Spiritual Gifts in 1 Cor 8:8," *Catholic Biblical Quarterly* 41 (1979), 292–98.

15. Guthrie, *op. cit.*, 146–54.

16. On the centrality of "Gospel" in Paul's understanding of his apostleship, see Schütz, *op. cit.*, 35–78.

17. Guthrie, *op. cit.*, points to Is 41:9–11. On Gospel in Paul and its connection to post-exilic traditions see J. A. Fitzmyer, "The Gospel in the Theology of Paul," *To Advance the Gospel* (New York: Crossroad, 1981), 149–61.

18. Horsley, "Consciousness," 377–86.

19. See the study of D. Lull, *The Spirit in Galatia: Paul's Interpretation of Pneuma as Divine Power* (Chicago: Scholars, 1979).

20. Lull, *op. cit.*, 53–95.

21. MacMullen, *Paganism*, 8, 112.

22. *Ibid.*, 47.

23. For a brief treatment of the problems in this passage see J. Murphy-O'Connor, *1 Corinthians*, 69f. Murphy-O'Connor properly points out that widespread social revolution would have been unlikely. The operation of the system for freeing slaves left them bound to their former masters and sometimes to the master's family so that they were not entirely free.

24. Malherbe, *op. cit.*, 71–86.

25. G. Dautzenberg, *Urchristliche Prophetie: Ihre Enforschung, ihre Voraussetzungen im Judentum und ihre Struktur im ersten Korintherbrief* (Stuttgart: Kolhammer, 1975), 122–48, 228f.

26. Murphy-O'Connor, *1 Corinthians*, 122–25.

27. G. Bornkamm, *Early Christian Experience* (New York: Harper, 1969), 162–69.

28. Dautzenberg, *op. cit.*, 226.

29. *Ibid.*, 230–33.

30. *Ibid.*, 231f.

31. Malherbe, *op. cit.*, 22–24.

32. Dautzenberg, *op. cit.*, 232f.

33. H. Conzelmann, *1 Corinthians* (Philadelphia: Fortress, 1975), 237–39.

34. Dautzenberg, *op. cit.*, 246–51.

35. Conzelmann, *op. cit.*, 240–42.

36. B. Holmberg, *Paul and Power* (Philadelphia: Fortress, 1980), 105–16. Holmberg points out that individual leaders are presupposed elsewhere (cf. 1 Thess 5:13; Gal 6:6).

37. Dautzenberg, *op. cit.*, 291–98.

38. Conzelmann, *op. cit.*, 246; Dautzenberg, *op. cit.*, 272; and, with reservations, C. K. Barrett, *The First Epistle to the Corinthians* (New York: Harper, 1968), 332.

39. S. Pomeroy, *Goddesses, Whores, Wives and Slaves: Women in Classical Antiquity* (New York: Schocken, 1975), 199–212; MacMullen, *Paganism*, 109.

40. C. P. Jones, *The Roman World of Dio Chrysostom* (Cambridge: Harvard, 1978), 105.

41. Bornkamm, *op. cit.,* 129.
42. Conzelmann, *op. cit.,* 201f; Bornkamm, *op. cit.,* 140f.
43. Conzelmann, *op. cit.,* 202.
44. Bornkamm, *op. cit.,* 150–51.

Chapter Three

WOMEN AND MINISTRY

Introduction

We have already seen that women appear involved in evangelism, in acting as patrons of local communities and in the worship of the communities. Clearly, early Christianity was not a sect in which men and women were separate in their religious practices. The educated writers of antiquity looked down on petty artisans, people with no fixed place of business, peasants, slaves, women and children as people of "superstition." Their religious views were held in contempt.[1] Most if not all Christians would fit into this category. However, the opinion of the cultured minority at the top of the steep social pyramid hardly represents the life of most people. The Corinthian situation provides a striking example of the influence that the hierarchical patterning of society had on all levels. When historians ask questions about the role of women in religious cults and their devotion to particular deities, they are at the mercy of the inscriptional record. Women are less likely to leave a record of their names and vows in stone.[2] Consequently, we do not have reliable data about the roles of women in ancient religious cults. We cannot say that Christianity was more or less attractive to women than other groups.[3] However, as with the question of evangelization, we must make an effort to appreciate the position of women in the New Testament communities. Questions about the position of women are not the ideological preoccupation of the privileged minority in developed countries. A global change in the relationship between women and their social contexts is underway. This change is amply illustrated for the third world in R. Critchfield's twenty-year study of villages. Modernization at the village level is occurring and can alleviate the pressing problems of poverty and hunger. However, Critchfield found that the introduction of birth control, high yield grains and technology were not enough to bring about development. The role of women also had to change. Their equality did not have to take on the forms that it has in the industrialized West, but as the custodians of culture and the first educators of children, women did have to have the equality of rights and of education which enabled them to participate in the village revolution.[4]

No one can deny that the shifting roles of women in society have created a discrepancy between their experiences in the Church and outside it that did not exist when many of us were growing up. When I was ten the fact that I could not be a minister or an altar boy was merely a reflection of what I considered the real social injustices of the world—that I could not play little league baseball or take shop or wear pants to school. My experience with Church was not significantly different from my experiences elsewhere. For today's ten-year-old, that parallelism no longer exists. Churches which have not changed accordingly become conspicuous anomalies. But there is a more serious question behind the question of roles for women, which we hinted at in our introduction. It is the question of appropriate Church structure. We have enough experience of women leaders in business and professional fields to know that they have no special protection against being authoritarian, status conscious, biased and even politically corrupt. They could just as well become members of a hierarchical, clerical system, of the patriarchal church, as the next person. Thus, the pressing question about ministry is the question of what sort of Church we are to have.

The ecumenical movement of the past two decades has brought all Christians to be more aware of the genuine plurality of ministries. No single perception of the Gospel and discipleship can be said to limit God's saving activity. No single perception of the Gospel dictates a style of ministry which must be followed in all places at all times. We have already seen that evangelization has a very different face in different parts of the New Testament—indeed, even within Paul's own mission. Vatican II has suggested to Roman Catholics that ministry is to be viewed primarily as service to the people of God. It has also suggested that biblical understandings of Church and mission are to have the central place in the life and practice of the Church.[5]

We have already seen that the charismatic, wandering mission patterned on the life of Jesus was quite different from the official patterns of "priest" (from which Jesus and his disciples were excluded by descent) and "rabbi." Paul says that he must count his Pharisaic past as so much garbage when he comes to know Jesus (Phil 3:8). The first Christians had to piece together what authority in the community, what apostleship and what ministry would mean. They did not have a single sociological model to adopt.[6] Paul acknowledges that those who were apostles before him have some authority to ascertain whether or not he has been preaching in vain. Yet, he insists that his call comes directly from God. He expects communities that he has founded to acknowledge both his authority and that of certain associates whom he sends. Within the local communities people came to take up roles of service and of preaching the Gospel by different routes. Some may have come forth spontaneously; others appear to have been encouraged to do so by the apostle. However, there is enough evidence in Paul to show that particular individuals did hold positions of authority. They are most likely to have obtained those positions on the basis of service already rendered to the community. Such previously demonstrated ability to serve is presupposed when the qualifications for bishop and deacon are listed. But we cannot find in the earliest period any uniform process for creating identical communities. Indeed, as we have already seen, uniformity of that sort was not a goal of cultic associations in Graeco-Roman society.[7]

Diversity and the Roles of Women

The question about women and ministry in the New Testament cannot be solved by asking whether women are called "diakonos," "apostolos," or "fellow worker." They are so designated, but all of the terms are used in a very general fashion in Paul's letters. "Diakonos" can be applied to anyone who is traveling in the mission or serving the community. It can also be applied to the apostles. Paul says that Phoebe is "diakonos" of the community (Rom 16:1–2). The expression only tells us that she is engaged in some form of service to the Church. The social patterns of the time make it likely that she was the patron of a group which met in her house.[8] Rom 16:7 mentions Junia and Andronicus, presumably her husband, as "apostoloi." We have already seen that two women in Phil 4:2–3, Euodia and Syntyche, appear to have been missionaries of the association that Paul had formed with the Philippian community. They are said to have been among Paul's "fellow workers" in Asia Minor. The same may be intended by the reference to wives of Peter and other apostles in 1 Cor 9:5.[9]

Though the terminology does not permit us to attach specific offices to the women mentioned, their inclusion seems to be taken as a matter of course. Therefore, it seems reasonable to assume that it reflects a situation which was widely accepted. Women involved in the luxury trades, like Lydia from Philippi (Acts 16:14), often traveled. They may also have engaged in evangelization among their associates. Paul's recommendation for Phoebe assumes that she is in business. Since men and women worked together in shops and trades, we may assume that the shops were also places in which others were brought into the community.[10] The roles attributed to women in the Pauline mission do not appear to be different from roles that such women might have filled in society generally. As is the case for the men mentioned in the same contexts, there is no evidence of the formal commissioning of such persons. They all belong to the groups which Paul calls "co-workers." Ellis' study of the terminology which Paul applies to this group suggests that perhaps "diakonos" has a more precise meaning and designates persons who are engaged in preaching or teaching whether as missionaries or as workers in local congregations. Further, Gal 6:6 implies that this type of worker deserves to be paid by the community.[11] Certainly, the Philippian association supported those who were missionaries on its behalf. Paul's own practice clearly varied from place to place. He does not demand pay when he is working to support himself. 1 Cor 9:6 associates Barnabas with the same policy of working rather than accepting pay. We cannot draw any uniform picture of how different communities and those who preached and taught there were related financially. However, nothing in the evidence allows us to presume that only men were "real diakonoi," paid teachers. Women like Phoebe, who appear to be wealthy enough to serve as patrons, would clearly not be paid any more than male patrons would be. Paul's workshop environment suggests that the distinctions were more economic and social than sexual. Indeed, such a mode of life appears to have contributed to the contempt in which he was held by some of the Corinthians.[12]

In addition to the co-workers, a more limited group appears in the Pauline correspondence. These are the people who are referred to as "brothers" and who are often sent with Paul's authority or are associated with Paul in the greeting of a letter.[13] They have the authority to formally represent the apostle. Such representation has legal overtones. Timothy and Titus can substitute for the absent apostle in *societas* relationships.[14] Later tradition in the Pauline churches represented by the pastoral epistles makes Timothy and Titus the models for the office of "overseer" (*episkopos*) of the local community, a somewhat different position than that Timothy and Titus enjoyed as representatives of the apostle traveling from one community to another. Women were not permitted to act in such a legal capacity, so it is hardly surprising that there are none in this special group of Pauline co-workers. Nor would women patrons be able to represent their local communities in legal actions or in pleading the case of the local community before an imperial official. They were not able to participate in the public life of their communities as male patrons could. Consequently, it is hardly surprising—and not necessarily drawing back from a freer position during the earlier period— that when the community consolidates around publicly visible representatives, those representatives are men. Such persons are to head the house churches in which the community will meet and are to be respected members of the local community (1 Tim 3:4–12).[15]

Many exegetes point to 1 Tim 3:11 as evidence that women continued to have an official role in the local congregation. The instructions being offered to "diakonoi" are generalized to apply to women: "Likewise, the women must be serious, not slanderers but temperate, faithful in all things." Some interpreters assume that the author is addressing wives of deacons. Others point out that there is no parallel in the instructions for bishops. They conclude that the parallelism between verses 8 and 11 implies that the author is speaking of women deacons.[16] Or the instruction may envisage some form of joint ministry such as that referred to in Rom 16:7.[17] Whether wives, independent women deacons or joint ministers with their husbands, this passage does indicate that there were women who continued to exercise some officially recognized ministerial role in the Pauline communities after the formalization of leadership in those churches around the *episcopos*. Other passages in the pastoral epistles which assert commonly held views about women's place should not be read as legalistic retrenchment any more than common ethical platitudes give us a true picture of women in the society as a whole.

Women Prophets—Speaking in the Assembly

Social conventions held that women did not speak in legal or political assemblies. Rules which prohibit them from speaking in public in the New Testament follow the conventions of the period. Both 1 Cor 14:33b–36 and 1 Tim 2:8—3:1a have taken common ethical preaching about the duties of members of a household and applied it to the rules for the worshiping community. The household structure of early Christian communities gives such ethical teaching a prominent place. Comments on modesty in feminine dress and the subordination of wives and children are stock topics. Inscriptions praise women for their seemly behavior. Both 1 Cor 14 and 1 Tim 2 appear to have emerged in response to abuses within particular communities. 2 Tim 3:6 hints that women are prominent among the false teachers whom the author wishes to keep from gaining a following in the community.[18] 1 Cor 14:33b–36 is frequently thought to be an interpolation of a later rule into Paul's discussion. If so, the context, regulating the use of ecstatic gifts in worship, does not tell us about the situation under which the rule came into force in the Pauline churches. Exegetes suggest that such rules are the result of increased Jewish Christian influence in the Pauline communities after Paul had left Asia Minor.[19] A general editing of the Pauline letters for use in those communities brought together materials which would support the growing concerns for "good order." The same concerns lead to the increasing use of the "household code" ethic in Col, Eph, the pastorals and non-Pauline letters like 1 Pet.[20]

However they developed, the restrictions on the public speaking of women cannot tell the whole story. Tit 2:4–5 gives older women the task of instructing the younger. Presumably the instruction referred to is pre-baptismal catachesis. Women also engaged in praying and prophesying. The daughters of Philip were known as prophetesses (Acts 2:9). Women also appear to have been teachers in some Pauline churches (Acts 18:26). The activities of preaching, that is, exhortation, and prophesying are closely related as we have seen.[21] 1 Cor 11:3–16 is our earliest evidence for men and women praying and prophesying in the Christian assembly. Some commentators have come to hold that it represents a later interpolation. They point out that it breaks into a chain of arguments about behavior at meals and tightly knit allusions to the Exodus traditions. They note that the argument is awkward and appears to use non-Pauline language.[22] We concur with those who still feel that this passage is original with 1 Cor. The peculiarities of language, like those elsewhere in 1 Cor, may derive from the peculiarities of the Corinthian situation, especially their interest in Adam typology. Paul has already broken into his meal sequence with the discussion about apostolic authority in 1 Cor 9. Further, if 1 Cor 14:33b–36 was an interpolation, the interpolator must have assumed that the prophesying related in chapter 14 included women as it does here.[23]

Paul structures the argument of this passage as he does his other arguments about liturgical order. He begins by stating the principle of the situation and the situation that he wishes to correct at Corinth (vv 3–12). In this case, he opposes certain fashions of dress among women (and men) who are praying or prophesying in the assembly. Then he establishes a rule which he expects the community to follow (vv 13–15). Finally, he concludes with an appeal to authority and the customs of other communities (v 16). It is also typical that Paul's actual rules tend to come from social convention rather than from the theological considerations directly. He makes that approach quite clear when he states the rule that women are to pray with head covered and then follows it up with an appeal to "what nature teaches." Such appeals are commonplaces of popular ethical preaching. Nature in this context has nothing to do with the earlier discussion of order in creation.

The theological section of the passage contains several eliptical expressions, which must be supplied by the translator:

> I wish you to know that the head of every man is Christ; the head of woman, the man; the head of Christ, God. Every man praying or prophesying having (something hanging) down from his head disgraces his head.

> Every woman praying or prophesying with uncovered head disgraces her head—she might as well be shaven. For if a woman is not covered, she should be shaven; but if it is a disgrace for a woman to be shaven or shorn, she should be covered.

> But a man should not cover his head, since he is the image and glory of God. Woman is the glory of man. For man is not from woman but woman from man. Man was not created through the woman but woman through the man.

> Therefore, the woman ought to have (a sign of?) au-
> thority on her head because of the angels—in any
> case (there is) not woman without man nor man with-
> out woman in the Lord. For as the woman (came into
> being) through the man, so now the man through the
> woman—but all things are from God. (1 Cor 11:3–12)

Paul is presuming that the Corinthians are familiar with Jewish traditions of interpreting Genesis in which Adam is the
image of God, that is, the archetype of humanity. He returns
to this theme in 1 Cor 15:20–49 to counter Corinthian denial of
the resurrection with the image of the risen Christ as the true
image of God, the spiritual Adam.[24] Paul adds Christ to that
order of creation in the beginning of the passage. Presumably,
some of the abuses in the Corinthians' behavior derived from
their claims to be "in Christ." Paul asserts that although the
distinction between men and women does not matter "in the
Lord," the order of creation is still to be respected.

The difference of dress between men and women reflects
the order of creation. However, the "authority" on the head of
the woman who is praying or prophesying is to be respected
even by the angels.[25] Paul seems most concerned with the activities of women. Though he also rejects certain behavior by
men, the final rule lays more emphasis on the women's dress
than on the men's.[26] Pointing to the fact that we have no evidence for women being heavily veiled in public, Murphy-
O'Connor suggests that "veiling" simply refers to women
having their hair dressed in conventional style, which would
include some covering or net.[27] It would not be loose or flying
about in the manner of ecstatic prophetesses. The "shorn
head" is not an alternative. It is meant to be ironic and perhaps a reference to a degrading punishment suffered by slaves
or prisoners of war. The peculiar reference to something hang-
ing down from a man's head may not have anything to do with

a head covering but refer to the possibility of a man growing long hair and treating it like a woman's. Such a practice is also widely condemned in popular philosophic preaching. The man should cut his hair and not be half man/half woman.[28] We cannot be certain exactly what the situation was at Corinth. Paul's attempt to order relationships between men and women both in view of the new creation, "in the Lord," in which they are equally dependent on each other and on God and in view of the created order suggests that the Corinthian actions were predicated on the basis of the new situation of being "in the Lord." Paul brings the eschatological reservation into play here as he does with the questions about spiritual gifts. Being "in the Lord" has not removed Christians from this creation into the new one. Christian freedom permits the woman who is inspired by the Spirit to prophesy a sign of authority, which even the angels recognize. Christian obedience respects the order established in God's creation.

The New Creation: Equality in Christ

Paul himself acknowledges the tradition of equality "in Christ."[29] The image of an eschatological renewal which obliterates the distinctions that separate humans appears to have been part of the pre-Pauline baptismal tradition. Paul quotes a formula to that effect in Gal 3:27–28:

> For as many of you as were baptized into Christ have put on Christ. There is neither Jew nor Greek; there is neither slave nor free; there is neither male nor female, for you are all one in Christ.

The formula in Galatians indicates liturgical practice. It does not indicate how such practice was, if at all, translated into the social life of the community. Anthropological examples show that while ritualized reversal of or freedom from social roles and constraints is common in many rites and festivals, that reversal does not carry over into the social sphere.[30] Paul does not think that slaves must become free as a matter of religious policy (1 Cor 7:17–24). In the same passage, he also points out that circumcision/uncircumcision are indifferent. A Gentile who becomes a Christian does not have to be circumcised; a Jew does not have to remove the marks of circumcision. The passages in which Paul insists on removing the distinction between Jew/Gentile refer to those who would insist that Gentile Christians join Israel in the physical sense by being circumcized and keeping kosher.[31] Thus, evidence suggests that the equality of all "in Christ," which is a sign of the new creation, was not understood to be a project that was to be translated into the social sphere of the old creation. It did apply in the religious sphere in that Paul insists that salvation does not require persons to change their status from what it was when they converted ("their calling"). From the perspective of the Galatians, this assertion of the order of things represents freedom for the Gentile Christians to continue as such.[32]

The formula "neither male nor female" derives from the same type of Genesis exegesis that underlies 1 Cor 11:3–16. Jewish exegetes distinguished between the two creations, that in Gen 1:27 and in Gen 2:7. The former, they said, refers to the divine image by which humans are like God. That image is androgynous, neither male nor female, and immortal. The second account refers to the creation of humans as embodied beings. As such, they belong to one sex or another and are subject to the natural process of mortality, the dissolution of body and soul.[33] Here is an example of such exegesis:

By this (=Gen 2:7) he (=Moses) shows very clearly the vast difference between the man so formed and the one who came into existence earlier according to the image of God: for the man so formed is an object of sense perception, already having certain qualities, consisting of body and soul, being man or woman, and by nature mortal. But the one after the (divine) image was an idea, a type, a seal, a concept, *incorporeal, neither male nor female, by nature incorruptible.*[34]

When Christians make use of liturgical formulae of this sort (also 1 Cor 12:13; Col 3:11), they are affirming that Christ is the one who brings humanity to the true image of God, to its created immortality.[35] The divisions between people which we experience in this world are signs of mortality. They are overcome by the Spirit which restores the true image of God in humanity, "neither circumcision nor uncircumcision but a new creation" (Gal 6:15).[36]

Political use of the androgynous imagery in antiquity presents an ideal of humanity united in a single polity. Paul's image of the Spirit uniting the Christian community in a single body is related to such traditions. He combines it with another of the unity formulas in 1 Cor 12:12–13:[37]

For as the body is one and has many members, all the members of the body while many are one body, thus also Christ. For we all in one Spirit have been baptized into one body, whether Jew or Greek, whether slaves or free, and we have all drunk one Spirit.

Thus, Christians might well have claimed that this ideal was realized in their community.[38] However, it is important to recognize that such ideals were seen as visions against which people measured the imperfections in existing social arrangements. They were not perceived as blueprints for utopian social experimentation. Some exegetes think that perhaps Paul found the Corinthians trying to actualize the obliteration of distinctions and boundaries in their lives. His assertions about the proper respect for order reject such claims to live out of the fullness of the new age by destroying the boundaries inherent in this age. The divisive consequences of the Corinthian experiment may even have led Paul to draw back from the use of symbols of unity, freedom and transcendence of boundaries in later writings.[39]

Whatever one makes of Paul's problems at Corinth, the general outlines of the Pauline position seem clear. Elements of subordination and hierarchy are built into creation. Jesus himself is "under" God. Therefore, the various forms of social order which reflect the ordering of creation are to be supported. Subordination of one person to another is not *a priori* evil. Second, drawing on Genesis exegesis as well, the image of God in the human person cannot be said to be either male or female. Sexual distinctions apply to this perishable material world, not to the spiritual world. Consequently, the renewal of that image made possible through the Spirit has nothing to do with a person's sexual, social or ethnic status. The image of Christ, the spiritual Adam, to which all will be conformed in the resurrection (1 Cor 15:20–23, 45–49), is the same for all baptized Christians. Third, God is the only one who gives spiritual gifts to members of the body. Women may be given the gifts of prayer and prophecy as well as men. What is under the control of the community is how these gifts are used. They must be used in such a way as to build up the community. As we saw in the last chapter, Paul even presumes that some people will refrain from using certain spiritual gifts for the greater benefit of the whole. Paul consistently argues that exhibitions of Christian freedom which violate the "good order" of the communities in which Christians live cannot contribute to "building up" the body of Christ. However, he does not suppose that the arrangements dictated by society and custom are graven in stone. They are part of a world which is passing away. Paul does not envisage the problems which Christians might face in situations in which the consensus about proper behavior is radically different from his own. However, as exegetes have frequently pointed out, Paul often demonstrates a willingness to determine what Christian behavior ought to be on a case by case basis. He recognizes that certain essentials for salvation in the Jewish community do not have to be required of Gentile Christians. He even reapplies the sayings of Jesus to his own situation in a way that could hardly be considered literal interpretation.[40] Similar processes of discernment have to be applied in our own situation.

The Christian Widows: A Life of Service

Some people seem to have concluded that since the Spirit restored the true image of God in humans, people should no longer be subject to the passions of the body. 1 Cor 7 hints that Christians at Corinth had concluded that they should avoid all sexual relationships (also see 2 Cor 5:17).[41] Second- and third-century Gnostics gave ascetic interpretations of the sayings of Jesus, which reject all bodily passions as chains binding the soul to the evil, material world. Women as the object of sexual passion become the symbol of such bondage. Some interpreters think that such an asceticism was already finding its way into Pauline churches when the pastoral epistles were written. The claim that women are saved through childbirth, if they are Christians (1 Tim 2:13–15), was not an attempt to enslave women to the biology of reproduction. It was an attempt to protect women and families from the consequences that such an ascetic theology might have if it were adopted by men. Christianity stands on the side of preserving the family relationships on which society is built.[42] Murphy-O'Connor suggests that Paul's reference to Jesus' prohibition of divorce in 1

Cor 7:10–11 was directed to a situation in which a woman's husband sought to dissolve the marriage for ascetic reasons. She is not to accept such an arrangement willingly, but, if forced into it, to remain unmarried or be reconciled with her husband.[43]

In line with this general concern to maintain the structures of the family, the pastoral epistles provide for a special class of women: widows. They would later become models for Christian ascetic women. Anyone familiar with life in a tradtional society will recognize the problem facing women with no family to take them in. Since conversion frequently alienated Christians from their natural families, Christian women might find themselves at a special disadvantage. 1 Tim seeks to have the Christian community replace what such women have lost. This new order of women is not to be abused by those families who simply do not wish to support a widowed relative (1 Tim 5:3–16):

> Widows, honor those who are widows. But if a widow has children or grandchildren, let them learn piety toward their own household first and to repay those who begot them, for this is proper behavior before God. A real widow, who is left alone, hopes in God and continues to make supplications and prayers day and night; but the self-indulgent is dead even while she lives. Command these things so that they may be blameless. If someone does not provide for his own, especially his own household, he has denied the faith and is worse than an unbeliever. Let a widow be enrolled if she is at least sixty, has been the wife of one husband, and has become known for good deeds, for example raising children, showing hospitality, washing the feet of the saints, relieving those who are afflicted, being devoted to every good work. But not

younger widows, for when they grow restive against Christ, they wish to marry, and incur condemnation for having broken their first pledge; besides they become idle, flitting from house to house; and not only idle but gossips and busybodies who say what they should not. So I wish younger women to marry, bear children, rule over their households, and not give the enemy any opportunity to slander us. For some have already strayed after Satan. If a believing woman has (relatives who are) widows, let her aid them and not burden the Church, so that it may aid those who are real widows.

The image of the Christian widow is drawn from the stories of Anna and Judith, pious women who spent their time in prayer and good works. Those enrolled must have no other means of support. Like bishops and deacons, they must also have distinguished themselves in lives of service. 1 Tim is concerned to protect the community from the malicious gossip that might surround this new arrangement in the larger community. Christians might well be accused of using such women for immoral purposes. The qualifications of service, good works and prayer make it clear that those enrolled as widows also serve the community. Not only are they rescued from poverty and degradation, they are permitted to continue the lives of Christian service that they had already set out for themselves.[44] "Wife of one husband" parallels the requirement for bishops and deacons. Inscriptions on tombstones praise women who remain faithful to the memory of their husbands and do not remarry as was the custom.[45] However, 1 Tim does not encourage younger women to adopt such a life. Though some women today are incensed at the image of women presented in this passage, the author implies that it represents the experience which people in that community have already had.[46] Further, condemnation of "idleness" and "being a busybody" is general ethical teaching which is equally well applied to male members of the community elsewhere.[47]

The creation of an order of widows does represent an example in which Christians deal with the problems of a group of Christian women in a new way. They are not being enrolled in contrast to or criticism of the normal patterns of marriage and family life. Indeed, the organization of this group goes out of its way to see that those patterns are retained and that all Christians recognize their obligations to assist members of their own families. But there are other women who really have no one. These women, whose lives have already demonstrated their impeccable Christian character, are given a place of honor in the community. Their service is acknowledged and allowed to continue. They are freed from the poverty and contempt which would otherwise be their fate.

Summary

Clearly, the picture of women and ministry in Christian communities which emerges from the New Testament cannot be forced into any one of the ideological camps that presently divide Christians. Those who want support for a clerical system which prohibits women from assuming roles within the Church that are now acceptable behavior in the larger society cannot claim the New Testament as their sponsor. Those who want an ideology of women's liberation that would call women to break out of the social roles and obligations of marriage, family, and acceptable behavior in the name of their spiritual equality with men will not find the New Testament their sponsor either. Can God call women to minister, even to pray and prophesy, in the Christian community? Certainly. Can those gifts be ordered according to rules set by the community, which are at least partially responsive to the particular social conditions in which Christians live? Necessarily. Are there situations in which the Church must create something new to affirm and support the lives of service led by Christian women, who would otherwise be destitute or held in contempt? Clearly.

The New Testament writers present us with their experience of community and of society and of women's activities in both. Their reflections on and rules about the activity of Christian women are directly related to the social situation in which particular men and women are living and working. They are also responsible to those outside the community in that Christian behavior must not become a roadblock for the Gospel. Evangelization and building up the body of Christ continue to be concerns which are reflected in the way in which Paul and others approach the problems of women. We live in quite a different time. Women have quite different roles, opportunities and obligations in our society. That experience should be part of the Christian discernment about women in ministry, women in families, social problems and the like. Some women are frustrated because they have gifts that they would like to put at the service of the community but cannot. The New Testament leaves us in that hard place of admitting that the community may refuse a gift. Spiritual gifts are not self-authenticating. Some may choose other Christian communities in which their particular gifts are sought out and affirmed. Even more women are frustrated at a more fundamental level. Neither the right nor the left appears willing to speak out of the experiences of women living in the societies of the twentieth century. 1 Tim did not invent the Christian widow and then find some women to fit the bill. The complex problem of widows was there in the community. 1 Tim sought to hear and resolve that problem in a Christian way, making use of all of the available social resources of the time. The various forms of ministry in which women engage in the Pauline mission are extensions of their talents and experiences in society at large. They are now able to use them for the Gospel.

If we are to have a community of adult Christians, we must recover the combination of experience and reflection on the Christian life that we find in the New Testament. We must learn to discern how the Spirit is building up the people of God in our own time. Then, perhaps, we will find the apostles of today writing the open and encouraging letters of recommendation for women who serve the community that Paul sends with Phoebe:

> I commend to you our sister, Phoebe, a deaconess of the church at Cenchreae, that you may receive her in the Lord as befits the saints, and help her in whatever she may require from you, for she has been a helper of myself as well. (Rom 16:1–2)

Notes

1. MacMullen, *Paganism,* 8.
2. *Ibid.,* 116f. MacMullen notes that the evidence for the beliefs of local, native populations is even harder to recover than that for immigrant women.
3. Therefore, one should be a little less enthusiastic about proclaiming Christianity as a new liberation for women; for the latter approach, see H. Kee, *Christian Origins in Sociological Perspective* (Philadelphia: Westminster, 1980), 88–90.
4. R. Critchfield, *Villages* (New York: Doubleday, 1981), 321–39.
5. A Lemaire, *Les Ministères aux origines de l'église* (Paris: Èditions du Cerf, 1971), 9–12.
6. Hence the failure of any effort to account for the use of "apostolos" in Paul on the basis of some earlier Jewish or Hellenistic model. See Schütz, *op. cit.,* 22–34.
7. On the Pauline evidence, see Holmberg, *op. cit.,* 9–11, 99–109, 120f, 180f.

8. On the difficulty of attaching the various terms to "offices," see Lemaire, *op. cit.,* 81–98.

9. See R. Gryson, *The Ministry of Women in the Early Church* (Collegeville: Liturgical Press, 1976), 5. Murphy-O'Connor, *1 Corinthians,* 86, argues that on its own merits 1 Cor 9:5 only asserts the right to be married and, consequently, to support for one's family.

10. On men and women working together in trades like weaving, see Pomeroy, *op. cit.,* 199f; on the workshop as a setting for evangelization see Hock, *op cit.,* 37–42.

11. E. Ellis, "Paul and His Co-Workers," *New Testament Studies* 17 (1971), 440–44.

12. Hock, *op. cit.,* 50–65.

13. Ellis, *op. cit.,* 445–48.

14. Sampley, *op. cit.,* 111.

15. O. Bangerter, *Frauen in Aufbruch: Die Geschichte einer Frauenbewegung in des Alten Kirche* (Neukirchener: Neukircher-Vluyn, 1971), 24.

16. Bangerter, *op. cit.,* 61f; Gryson, *op cit.,* 7f; M. Dibelius and H. Conzelmann, *The Pastoral Epistles* (Philadelphia: Fortress, 1972), 58.

17. Lemaire, *op cit.,* 134.

18. Dibelius-Conzelmann, *op cit.,* 44–49.

19. Bangerter, *op. cit.,* 30–35.

20. G. W. Tromf, "On Attitudes Toward Women in Paul and Paulinist Literature: 1 Cor 11:3–16 and Its Context," *Catholic Biblical Quarterly* 42 (1980), 196–215. Tromf thinks that 1 Cor 11:3–16 is also a post-Pauline interpolation indicative of Jewish Christian influence in the Pauline churches at the time when the Pauline letters were edited for general circulation.

21. Dautzenberg, *op. cit.,* 228–33.

22. For those who argue that 1 Cor 11:3–17 is an interpolation see W. O. Walker, "1 Corinthians 11:2–16 and Paul's Views Regarding Women," *Journal of Biblical Literature* 94 (1975), 94–110; L. Cope, "1 Cor 11:2–16: One Step Further," *Journal of Biblical Literature* 97 (1978), 435f; Tromf, *op cit.,* 196–99.

23. J. Murphy-O'Connor, "The Non-Pauline Character of 1 Corinthians 11:2–16?" *Journal of Biblical Literature* 95 (1976); 615–21; and responding to his critics, *idem,* "Sex and Logic in 1 Cor 11:2–16," *Catholic Biblical Quarterly* 42 (1980), 482–500.

24. See the discussion of the exegetical background to the Adam imagery in 1 Cor 15 by R. Horsley, "How Can Some of You Say That

There Is No Resurrection of the Dead? Spiritual Elitism in Corinth," *Novum Testamentum* 20 (1978), 216–25.

25. The role of the angles is hotly contested. J. Fitzmyer, "A Feature of Qumran Angelology and the Angles of I Cor. xi 10," *Essays on the Semitic Background of the New Testament* (London: Chapman, 1971), 187–204, points to the exclusion of anyone with a blemish from the Essene assembly because of the presence of angels. Other interpreters look for a background more closley related to the Genesis tradition. J. Meier, "On the Veiling of Hermeneutics (1 Cor 11:2–16)," *Catholic Biblical Quarterly* 40 (1978), 220f, suggests that the lustful angels of Gen 6:2 are the ones intended. He argues that the tradition of Christian superiority to the angels in 1 Cor 6:3 (and Col/Eph) makes it unlikely that they would control liturgical celebration. Tromf, *op cit.*, 207–209, agrees that the passage cannot refer to the Essene views because it does not presuppose some flaw in women. He looks to Jewish traditions about Adam and Eve which require that women show extra repentance in the presence of God and the angels.

26. Conzelmann, *1 Corinthians*, 182–91.

27. Murphy-O'Connor, "Sex and Logic," 487–90.

28. *Ibid.*, 485–87; see, for example, Epictetus, *Discourses* 3.1, 30–31.

29. Tromf, *op. cit.*, 211, follows this line in Pauline exegesis, "Paul is certainly a clear voice asserting the freedom and equality of women within the eschatological community."

30. Tromf, *op. cit.*, 213f, points out that ecstatic prophecy enhances the self-esteem of women in African tribes where a prophetess may be accepted as a mouthpiece of the divine. However, this religious status does not bring about a leveling of the positions of men and women generally.

31. See the discussion of the argument and context of this passage in Gal in Stendahl, *op cit.*, 17–22. C. K. Barrett, *op cit.*, 168–72, treats the relevant passage in 1 Cor. He makes two important points (1) no one in Corinth appears to have raised the question about whether Gentiles should be circumcised; (2) Paul presumes that the converted Jew will continue to follow the Torah. Stendahl, *op cit.*, 2, also points out that Paul never calls Jewish Christians to abandon Judaism. For a general survey of the use of the "neither male nor female formula" see B. Witherington, "Rite and Rights for Women— Galatians 3:28," *New Testament Studies* 27 (1981), 593–604. Witherington thinks that Paul is using the formula to resist pressure from

the Judaizers to have women marry and adopt a subordinate place in the community.

32. Thus, Paul's use of the formula does not support the view that he is concerned with a principle of women's rights as such.

33. See W. Meeks, "The Image of the Androgyne: Some Uses of a Symbol in Earliest Christianity," *History of Religions* 33 (1974), 182.

34. Philo of Alexandria, *On Creation,* 134.

35. H. D. Betz, *Galatians* (Philadelphia: Fortress, 1979), 182.

36. *Ibid.,* 189.

37. Barrett, *op. cit.,* 286–90.

38. Betz, *op. cit.,* 190–95.

39. *Ibid.,* 200.

40. Meier, *op. cit.,* 212–216, points to a hermeneutical "double standard" in the Declaration on Women and the Priesthood. The Declaration admits that 1 Cor 11:2–16 belongs to Paul's adaptation to a particular cultural tradition but refuses to apply the same considerations to other passages.

41. Betz, *op cit.,* 197–98.

42. Dibelius-Conzelmann, *op cit.,* 45–47.

43. Murphy-O'Connor, *1 Corinthians,* 62–64.

44. Gryson, *op. cit.,* 9f.

45. Bangerter, *op cit.,* 47f.

46. And not notably different from the presuppositions about male sexuality in 1 Cor 7:2–9.

47. See the condemnation of idleness and busybodies among Christians in 1 Thess 4:11; 2 Thess 3:6–13; on the ethical background to this passage, see Malherbe, *op cit,* 23–27.

Chapter Four

CHRISTOLOGY AND THE MINISTRY OF RECONCILIATION

Introduction

Many people see little connection between the contemporary arguments of theologians over Christology which occasionally make the religion section of *Time* and the sweeping changes in the image of the Church and the activities of Christians which are more common fare in those pages. They may be equally baffled by the activism of clergy in Latin America and the increasing visibility of fundamentalism at home. Yet, all are efforts that express our need to recover the effective presence of Christianity in the public sphere. Purely individual and private visions will not guide us through the troubling conflicts of values that tear at our world. It is often forgotten that theology has other audiences beyond the scholarly academy. Theologians are not seeking to construct individual, private systems. Their job finally is to articulate the significance of the Gospel for and through the experiences of the larger Christian community. Nor is their task purely Church-oriented. They must also seek to address that same Christian vision to the shared concerns of humanity, to "the public."[1]

As theologians turn to the question of Jesus, they seek to understand how Jesus may be said to mediate salvation in the concrete situations of today's world. The question about Jesus is always a question about the meaning of salvation. That question cannot be answered in identical terms from one age to the next, since it must address the specifics faced by people in each age. We face our world with a painful awareness of the complex influence on human life and behavior of social, political, economic, psychological and historical conditions. We know that the balance between humanity, technology and nature is so precarious that it could be upset to the point at which nature would no longer recover. We know the perils of nuclear war which could wipe the human species from the globe and perhaps from the cosmos. Our religious imagery has yet to catch hold of the terrifying images of self-extermination because they disrupt the natural continuities in which humans have expressed the conviction of immortality.[2]

The theologian cannot ignore the contemporary crisis of religious symbolism. With all the horrors of the modern dynamics of victimization and annihilation, Christians must find the significance of the affirmation, "Christ died for our sins."[3] Sometimes people simply identify Jesus as one in a long line of victims. The Christian confession that Jesus is human-divine reveals the inadequacy of such an image. The New Testament sees in Jesus a claim about God; as one theologian has put it, in Jesus we learn that "God is Jesus-like."[4] Such a God is not an abstract, cosmic power which overwhelms the human world and its imperfections. Rather, we find God identifying with that world, suffering the consequences of its imperfections. God will not relieve the anxieties of a post-nuclear world by promising a stronger power to prevent the abuse of powers misused by human sinfulness.

Jesus and His Death

For the Christian to claim that Jesus' death shows us God, that death must be more than a judicial accident, more than another innocent victim, more than martyrdom for a cause. The New Testament shows us a variety of images in which early Christians tried to express their perception of what had happened in Jesus' death. The Gospels picture the difficulties of Jesus' disciples in grasping why Jesus—and, through him, God—became involved in human suffering. Unless Jesus' own relation to death had something of this quality of divine involvement, the claim that through his death God's salvation is mediated to a sinful world makes God a sadist who manipulates the innocent.

Several of Jesus' sayings relate death and service in a way that is not simply reading back into Jesus' time the fact of his death. The connection is made in three independent traditions—Mk 10:42–45, Lk 22:24–27 and Jn 13:1–20.[5] These sayings require that relationships among Jesus' disciples reverse the common patterns of society:

> You know that those who are supposed to rule over the Gentiles lord it over them, and their great men exercise authority over them. But it shall not be so among you; but whoever would be great among you must be your servant, and whoever would be first must be slave of all. For the Son of Man also came not to be served but to serve, and to give his life as a ransom for many. (Mk 10:42–45)
>
> A dispute also arose among them, which of them was to be regarded as the greatest. And he said to them, The kings of the Gentiles exercise lordship over them; and those in authority over them are called benefac-

tors. But not so with you; rather let the greatest among you become as the youngest and the leader as one who serves. For which is greater, one who sits at table, or one who serves? But I am among you as one who serves. (Lk 22:24–27)

Each version reflects the concerns and background of the evangelist. Mark identifies the servant-messiah with the suffering Son of Man. Luke shows a more sophisticated recognition of the function of hierarchical relationships in ancient society. The "benefactors" of society actually wield authority over others. We have already seen that some early Christians found it difficult to break that pattern. Yet, this tradition makes it clear that Jesus challenged the finely tuned balance of hierarchy and privilege on which ancient society was constructed. Further, the identification with the slave, the most despised of humanity,[6] suggests that there are no limits to that service, no point at which a disciple might pull back and say "No further." The Johannine version dramatizes this reversal in the footwashing scene.

Two other sayings instruct disciples that following the pattern set by Jesus is necessary for anyone who is to participate in the rule of God:

You are those who have continued with me in my trials; as my Father appointed a kingdom for me, so do I appoint for you that you may eat and drink at my table in my kingdom, and sit on thrones judging the twelve tribes of Israel. (Lk 22:28–30)

Truly, I say to you that I shall not drink again of the fruit of the vine until that day when I drink it new in the kingdom of God. (Mk 14:25)

Jesus' sayings about service show "making the great least" to be the key to the messianic rule of God. They present a coherent image of life under the rule of God in which even death is not meaningless. We cannot evaluate it in our categories, since it is the death of a person willing to be slave rather than master.[7] The question remains: What follows when such a death is perceived to speak the truth about the way in which God rules? God will not appear as the great one, the benefactor whose position and title permitted him to "lord it over" the masses of humanity. God cannot be demanding of humans the kind of groveling service which patrons could exact from their poor clients. God does not forgive our sins by participating in the dynamics of power.

Ministry of Reconciliation

One of the many images which early Christians used to capture the reality of salvation in Jesus was reconciliation. Christians today find that image a fruitful one because it suggests that the central experience of salvation reaches out into the many dimensions of our lives—personal, societal and even international. Thus, it may bring together some of the fragmented pieces of our experience. Such unities seem to be required lest fragmentation become deterioration and destruction. Some studies of Paul treat reconciliation as though it is a variant for justification by faith. However, the latter has been developed to meet the specific situation of including Gentiles in the people of God without requiring that they become members of Israel.[8] From the Jewish perspective, which divides humanity into Jew/Gentile, overcoming that boundary is a great act of reconciliation.[9] Consequently, reconciliation is applied to that situation, but it also opens out to other dimensions as well.[10]

The Pauline tradition develops the cosmic dimensions of the symbol. Rom 11:15 points to Jewish rejection of the Messiah as reconciliation for the Gentiles ("the world"). Their acceptance will bring the completion of the plan of salvation, the resurrection.[11] 2 Cor 5:17–20 develops the eschatological significance of Christ's death in another way. The Christian becomes part of the new creation, of the world which is now reconciled to God. Rom 5:10–11 points to reconciliation as the gift Christians have received through the death of Jesus, but, like Rom 11:15, it also points toward the future in which Christians are to share the "life" (= resurrection) of Jesus. The cosmic significance of this reconciliation is developed even further in Col 1:19–23 and Eph 2:14–16. Christ's death has broken down "the law" which divided Jew from Gentile and sinner from God. This cosmic event creates a new people of God. At the same time, as Col emphasizes, such a reconciliation can only be the work of God. It is possible because the "fullness of God" dwells in Jesus. 2 Cor 5:17–20 and Col 1:19–23 also present this message of reconciliation as a task for the life of the apostle. It must be preached to all creation. Consequently, reconciliation is dynamic. It is not a static guarantee of future salvation but a reality which defines how Christians live and act in the present. This symbolism encompasses the whole story of humanity: the sinful past which has been met by God's new act of salvation, the present in which salvation as reconciliation is realized, and the future when we will see the cosmic proportions of reconciliation.

As we saw in Chapter Two, biblical faith is built on human thanksgiving for the saving action of God. The reconciliation of the world with God is God's saving act. It is never the creation of humans. The Christian expression of reconciliation appears to be even more emphatic than Jewish parallels in stressing God's initiative in bringing about reconciliation.[12] Thus, we return to an important feature of the Christian image of God. God is involved in human suffering; he is not a passive spectator waiting for humans to extract themselves and return to obedience and faithfulness.[13] The revelation of God in Jesus is a revelation of God in relation to the world. Reconciliation is an important image of that relationship.

Romans 5:1–11

> Therefore, since we are justified by our faith, we have peace with God through our Lord Jesus Christ. Through him we have attained access to this grace in which we stand, and we rejoice in our hope of sharing the glory of God. More than that, we rejoice in our sufferings, knowing that suffering produces endurance, and endurance produces character, and character produces hope, and hope does not disappoint us, because God's love has been poured into our hearts through the Holy Spirit who has been given to us.
>
> While we were yet helpless, at the right time Christ died for the ungodly. Why, one will hardly die for a righteous person—though perhaps for a good person one will dare even to die. But God shows his love for us in that while we were yet sinners Christ died for us. Since, therefore, we are now justified by his blood, much more shall we be saved by him from the wrath of God. For if while we were enemies we were reconciled to God by the death of his Son, much more, now that we are reconciled, shall we be saved by his life. Not only so, but we also rejoice in God through our Lord Jesus Christ, through whom we have now received our reconciliation.

This passage brings together images of peace with God,[14] atonement, justification and reconciliation. The image of peace brings into play all the nuances of the Old Testament picture of salvation as *shalom*.[15] This section of Romans serves as preface to the long description of the Spirit working in and through the sufferings of the present time in 8:14–39.[16] Paul has oriented this introduction around the sources of confidence that Christians have in facing such sufferings. Again, the structure of the passage is characteristic of biblical thanksgiving. The overwhelming salvation experienced in the past, a saving death for those who are sinners and enemies of God, peace and reconcilation with God, serves to ground the certainty of future salvation. The reconciliation of humanity with God is expressed in the activity of the Spirit received in the present. Rom 8:18–27 makes it clear that the "groanings and weaknesses" of the present do not count as evidence against salvation. Though salvation will remain incomplete as long as the cosmos is not transformed, the sufferings experienced in the present are signs of the Spirit working. Therefore, endurance is not simply putting up with a troublesome world until God brings it to an end. Endurance and hope see the glory of God manifest even in the present time.[17] Those for whom reconciliation is a reality do not, then, have the same vision of the sufferings of the present world as others. Those sufferings show imperfection and the disastrous effects of human sinfulness, but they also bear witness to a longing for the transforming power of God, a longing that itself requires the working of the Spirit.

Romans 11:15

> For if their rejection means the reconciliation of the world, what will their acceptance mean but life from the dead.

Reconciliation and the associated experiences of peace with God and working of the Spirit are not matters of private religious experience. They are developed out of reflection on God's salvation in creating a people. When we privatize the biblical language of salvation, we lose the important connection between salvation and the existence of a human community which lives out of God's action, a community which would not exist without that action. Paul sees the new Christian community in which the people of God now includes Gentiles. In this section of Rom 11, Paul addresses the Gentiles. Salvation history would seem to have taken another disastrous turn for God's people. Early Christian preaching of the cross presented it as Israel's "no" to her Messiah, to God's eschatological salvation. God's "yes" to Jesus in the resurrection demonstrates that the "no" to the cross is a "no" to God's saving activity.[18] Here, Paul insists that the "no" of Israel does not end her place as God's people. It has provided the opportunity for the Gentiles to be included, but the final drama is to include the return of Israel to share in the messianic banquet.[19] The story of salvation is not finished until the "yes" which heralds the resurrection of the righteous and the final transformation of the cosmos.[20]

Ephesians 2:14–16

> For he is our peace, who has made us both one, and has broken down the dividing wall of hostility by abolishing in his flesh the law of commandments and ordinances, that he might create in himself one new man in place of two, so making peace, and might reconcile us both to God in one body through the cross, thereby bringing hostility to an end.

Ephesians elaborates on the theme of reconciliation of a humanity which had been divided by the law into Jew and Gentile. The "mystery" of God's salvation, which Paul as apostle to the Gentiles says has been revealed to him, is that God has a plan to bring salvation to the Gentiles. This plan did not repeat the messianic expectation that an obedient Israel might bring others to God, that is, the Gentiles would come under the law. Instead, reconciliation came through the cross (cf. Gal 1:12; Rom 11:25; Eph 3:6).[21] Reconciliation brings two hostile groups together in one body, a new human being. Since Jew/Gentile is a binary division of all humanity created by the law, the law itself is pictured as a wall that has been knocked down.

Those of us who do not structure the world in the binary categories Jew/Gentile, under the law/outside the law (=sinner), may find it difficult to appreciate the power of this image. God appears to have ripped apart the whole pattern of salvation in the cross and to have deprived the world of its fundamental ordering. Indeed, we often face a world in which we would be glad to only have two groups to deal with! Reconciliation must expand over even greater barriers and divisions. Instead of supposing that one must break down a single wall, we must deal with a complex web of conflicting claims and needs, of cultures and traditions. The imagery of the Spirit working through the groanings of creation may provide some encouragement for looking at the more complex situations facing reconciliation in our world.

2 Corinthians 5:17–20

> Therefore, if anyone is in Christ, he is a new creation; the old has passed away and, behold, the new has come. All this is from God, who through Christ reconciled us to himself, that is, God was in Christ reconciling the world to himself, not counting their trespasses against them, and entrusting to us the message of reconciliation. So we are ambassadors for Christ, God making his appeal through us on behalf of Christ: be reconciled to God.

We have already seen that reconciliation is not static. The "new creation" remains embedded in the old. Consequently, reconciliation becomes fundamental to the apostolic task. Notice that Paul is very careful in his description of that task. Reconciliation is a reality that is brought about by God. Humans have a place in making that appeal because for Paul the gospel which defines the life of the apostle is an extension of the saving activity of God in the cross.[22] But it is important to recognize that when Paul speaks in this way, he makes it clear that the extension is only possible through Christ. The apostle's mission of reconciliation can never be considered parallel to the "once for all" reconciliation of humanity and God in the cross.[23] This appeal to reconciliation in 2 Cor 5:19–20 is not an abstract statement of theological principle. Paul is asking the Corinthians, who have been alienated from the apostle by other Christian preachers and an unpleasant incident during Paul's last visit, to be reconciled to him. Paul is the one whose ministry brought them to reconciliation with God. Now they must overcome their hostility and be reconciled with Paul.[24]

Colossians 1:19–23

> For in him the fullness of God was pleased to dwell, and through him to reconcile to himself all things, whether on earth or in heaven making peace by the blood of his cross. And you who were once estranged and hostile in mind, doing evil deeds, he has now reconciled in his body of flesh by his death, in order to present you holy and blameless and irreproachable before him, provided you continue in the faith, steadfast and stable, not shifting from the Gospel you heard, which has been preached to every creature under heaven, and of which I, Paul, became a minister.

Colossians picks up this imagery of reconciliation as the foundation of the apostolic ministry. It presents the invitation to humanity to "be reconciled" as extended to the entire cosmos. Thus, reconciliation is not to be limited to the question of Jew/

Gentile in the people of God. Reconciliation is not limited to the problems facing Paul in his relationships with the Corinthian community. Nor is reconciliation simply a way of asserting the authority of the apostle in that situation. Reconciliation has cosmic dimensions. It is part of the "new creation" which comes into being with the death of Jesus. We saw in the last chapter that other expressions of unity, "neither Jew nor Gentile, slave nor free, male nor female," were used in the early baptismal liturgy to express the "new creation." Here, we find an image of that reconciliation as a cosmic event.[25] At the same time, we are again reminded that reconciliation grounds salvation and imparts a dynamic to Christian life. It does not permit Christians to rest on some false security. They must "continue steadfast in the Gospel." Ministry, which takes reconciliation as its foundation, then, must take that message to the polarities and divisions in concrete situations.

Reconciliation and Christian Consciousness

The biblical writers have constantly reminded us that we cannot rush into a situation and produce reconciliation. Christians today are painfully aware of the fact that external division and hostility has its internal counterpart. Consciousness and community are intertwined. Theologians have begun to ask whether there is a particular change of consciousness that is required of Christians. They recognize that the Bible does not address itself to our interiorizing, psychological questions.[26] Nevertheless, they argue that, given our understanding of the dynamics of the human psyche, we must ask what sort of human consciousness is implied by the biblical vision of the world. They begin seeking answers to this question by turning to the picture of Jesus himself.[27] For example, Thompson focuses on the images of Jesus in relationship to others.

Jesus appears as a radically related self. There is no concern to bolster or protect an independent ego. Rather, all of Jesus' relationships are characterized by radical openness. This openness to God led Jesus to a new intimacy with God as Father. His openness to other humans led him to accept enemies and sinners as friends. This same openness also led to a life of radical dependence on others. Jesus never isolates himself. His openness to women mirrors the same pattern. Thompson suggests that such relationships could only be sustained by a person who has reconciled the conflicting forces which divide the human person. For such a person, the other does not call forth defenses.[28]

Many psychological theories point to the reconciliation of masculine and feminine elements within the personality as the foundation of such integration.[29] Feminine imagery appears closely associated with the suffering/service side of discipleship. The one who renounces power as the mode of effective action must find other images for life than the crushing images of being destroyed by those who wield power. One of the most common is that of the woman giving birth. The woman of Rev 12 is such an example.[30] Jn 16:21 uses the image to console the disciples faced with the hour of Jesus' departure (cp. Is 26:16–19; 66:7–11). Closely related to these are images of women watching over those they love. Jn 19:26 takes that image of the women at the cross and embodies it in Jesus' mother and the beloved disciple. It recalls the imagery of divine protection from the mother's womb of Ps 22:9–10.[31] These images are not formulated by women for whom they might be part of the fabric of life but by men for whom they come to express the realities of discipleship.

Nor is this consciousness of the feminine side of discipleship limited to the Gospels. Paul draws upon feminine imagery at points of crisis in his relationships with different churches. To the Galatians who appear to be turning from his Gospel to Judaizing he writes:

> My little children, with whom I am again in labor until Christ be formed in you! I wish to be present with you now and to change my tone for I am perplexed about you. (Gal 4:19f)

The Corinthian community are like babes who must still be nursed, since they cannot eat solid food:

> But I, brethren, could not address you as spiritual people, but as fleshly people, as babies in Christ. I fed you with milk and not solid food, for you were not ready for it; and even yet you are not ready for you are still fleshly. For while there is jealousy and strife among you are you not still fleshly and behaving like ordinary people? (1 Cor 3:1–3)

However, such imagery is not simply called forth by crisis. It also describes the apostle's relationship to the congregation he founds. Paul explicitly contrasts his behavior among the Thessalonians, "gentle as a nurse taking care of her children," with the glory or rights that he might have demanded as an apostle (1 Thess 2:6–7).[32]

The Pauline examples make it clear that the required change in consciousness is necessary for the disciple to overcome the patterns of power and self-assertion which are an obstacle to the service envisaged in Jesus' sayings.[33] We can perceive the depths implied by such a reorientation if we follow Ong's suggestions about the implications of sociobiology.[34] Male identity has been formulated through ritualized patterns of conflict, necessary to separate from the enveloping matrix of the womb. Survival for females did not require such adaptive behavior. They must learn aggression only on behalf of what they have the responsibility to protect—home and children. Consequently, when females engage in conflict it is with a life and death seriousness quite different from the ritualized patterns of male behavior.[35] We live in a society which is moving away from the traditional arenas of ritualized aggression for males, such as academia and business. At the same time, women are entering these traditional areas of combat. The dismantling of ritualized patterns of aggression does not automatically mean that we will be better off even though studies have shown that the most aggressive individuals are not necessarily the most successful.[36] We could embrace a new Manicheism that would deny all rootedness in biologically differentiated metaphors;[37] we could find ourselves driven by root need for adversative relationships in order to establish identity and autonomy to uncontrolled outbreaks of aggression.[38] The contest meets the anxiety of an insecure ego by proving it able to master self and world. The consciousness which can move beyond the need to "grasp being like God" (Phil 2:6) to the nothingness of the slave must have secured its identity. Phil 2:6–11 pictures Jesus making that move out of the security of "being God." God, often identified with the masculine images of power and glory, the Creator, the one mighty in battle, the one against whom heaven and earth cannot stand, steps to the other side. The God who is Jesus-like emerges in suffering.

These reflections have many implications for those who are engaging in ministry. The question of male/female is not a simple problem of socially defined roles, since it is rooted in the development of the species. How we go beyond the socially encoded structures of conflict is as important as doing so. The Gospel images of Jesus as well as the latter patterns of imagery in and for the Church present deeply ambiguous combinations of struggle and passivity, of male and female that cut across our biological and social ones. God is Father because our relationship to God has the character of that of humans of both sexes to fathers: they can be deeply affectionate, a protective presence, but they are also "out there," less certainly part of us than our mothers. God is not, however, male. The biblical tradition has resisted all attempts to bring God into the biological order of images by supplying some feminine counterpart. Indeed, the only feminine counterpart emerges in Mary's "yes" (= the people of God), in a new gathering of human persons. Jesus himself presents a challenging paradox. He insists on suffering evil rather than resisting, yet engages in verbal combat with adversaries and, as the students always point out with great perplexity, overturns the money changers' tables. Knowing Christ and "the power of his resurrection" means sharing the *pathos* of the cross, Paul reminds us (Phil 3:10). Those who minister to such a community must find themselves challenged to move beyond the polarized consciousness, grounded in our biological development, to the realm of the spirit which empowers both struggle and passivity.[39]

Summary

Christianity has been entrusted with a vision of God reconciling the world to himself in Christ, from the position of servant, not conqueror. That vision is to mold the consciousness of those entrusted with the task of serving as "ambassadors" for that message. Such a task requires a community of adult men and women who are able to risk, to change, to assume responsibility, even to issue a challenge to others. They cannot retreat into private ghettos or communities of like-minded believers and suppose that they have attained the peace of Christ. A ministry of reconciliation seeks to be as active and as radically relational as Jesus. Paul links "new creation" to the ministry of reconciliation made effective in the life of the community by the apostle. John has the departing Christ found the community in the love command and entrust it with the mission to the world which he has from the Father. In a very real sense, the presence of God and Christ to that community depends upon its ability as a community to make reconciliation visible in the world at large.

The real danger of Christology is not in the possibility of some theoretical error. The real danger lies in the exploration of powerful religious symbols. It is the danger of the biblical God, always involved with humans in their history. That vision of God never allows us to rest within secure boundaries or, even, the familiar present. Ministry for such a God is never comfort, wholeness, or peace, in our sense of sinking below the tensions and conflicts of life (or "rising above" them). The God who is Jesus-like is not comfortable, not immutable, perhaps not whole, not powerful or authoritarian as human egos imagine. God is the small voice, the one hopelessly in love with a wayward people. The righteous cry out, but God does not bring this world to an end. Instead, the righteous are vindicated by the Spirit active in groans and weaknesses. This God has risked more than most of us could imagine—not only has he risked his Son; he continues to risk his creation. Hope may assure us that that risk is not a mistake; it does not absolve us from the responsibility for a ministry of reconciliation.

Notes

1. See the discussion of the three publics of the theologian in D. Tracy, *The Analogical Imagination* (New York: Crossroad, 1981), 3–46. Tracy points out that the "publicness" of theology stems from the fact that the questions about which theology speaks concern all people.

2. See R. Lifton, *The Broken Connection: On Death and the Continuity of Life* (New York: Simon and Schuster, 1979), 302–68.

3. R. Fuller, "Jesus Christ as Savior in the New Testament," *Interpretation* 35 (1981), 156.

4. W. Thompson, *Jesus Lord and Savior* (New York: Paulist, 1980), 113–15.

5. John has embedded this tradition in the footwashing scene; see P. Perkins, *The Gospel according to John* (Chicago: Franciscan Herald, 1978), 145–50.

6. Slaves were particularly despised since they could only survive through flattery and deceit; see MacMullen, *Social Relations,* 114–20.

7. Thompson, *op. cit.,* 67–71; Fuller, *op. cit.,* 146f.

8. Stendahl, *op. cit.,* 1–40.

9. Though non-Jews criticized Jewish exclusivism as "hatred of humanity," this binary symbolism, Jew/Gentile, would not have had the impact on a non-Jewish hearer that it would for a Jewish one. However, the other pairs, male/female and slave/free, would have made the point for a non-Jewish audience.

10. See J. Fitzmyer, "Reconciliation in Pauline Theology," *To Advance the Gospel,* 166–75.

11. Resurrection, here, does not refer to Jesus' resurrection but to the resurrection of the righteous at the parousia; see E. Kaesemann, *An die Römer* (Tübingen: C. B. Mohr (Paul Siebeck), 1974²), 294f.

12. Fitzmyer, *op. cit.,* 168. Fitzmyer points out that "reconciliation" language had to have developed among Greek-speaking Jews: 165; 182 n. 22 and n. 30.

13. This activity is reflected in the image of the divine suffering, *pathos;* see Thompson, *op. cit.,* 185.

14. Also see the combination of peace and the reconciliation of Jew/Gentile in Eph 2:11–18; Fitzmyer, *op. cit.,* 169.

15. Related expressions about Christ as "peace" in the Pauline tradition are Phil 4:7; 2 Thess 3:16; Col 3:15; see Fitzmyer, *op. cit.,* 182 n. 28.

16. See the discussion of the structure of this section of Romans by R. Byrne, "Living Out the Righteousness of God: The Contribution of Rom 6:1–8:13 to an Understanding of Paul's Ethical Presuppositions," *Catholic Biblical Quarterly* 43 (1981), 557–81.

17. J. Becker, *Paul the Apostle* (Philadelphia: Fortress, 1980), 146–49.

18. Fuller, *op. cit.,* 147f.

19. Stendahl, *op. cit.*, 28f.

20. Becker, *op. cit.*, 152f.

21. Stendahl, *op. cit.*, 28.

22. Schütz, *op. cit.*, 181f.

23. *Ibid.*, 205f.

24. F. Fallon, *2 Corinthians* (Wilmington: Michael Glazier, 1980), 51f.

25. Fitzmyer, "Reconciliation," 169–76.

26. See the protest against psychologizing Paul in Stendahl, *op. cit.*, 78–96.

27. Such statements are not claims about the "historical Jesus." They are based on seeing the Gospels as the symbols and founding narratives which arise from the event of Jesus. As such, the dynamics of those symbols and narratives show us the consciousness that develops in response to that event. On the Gospels as "Christian classic" and their relationship to the event of Jesus, see, Tracy, *op. cit.*, 248–304.

28. Thompson, *op. cit.*, 174–85.

29. C. Downing, *The Goddess: Mythological Images of the Feminine* (New York: Crossroad, 1981), 9–29. Downing challenges those theories which suppose that male/female operate as poles on the same level. She finds the quest for the feminine in the more primordial images of "the mother," that from which we all emerge, and into which all dissolves at death. As an attempt to answer her challenge to Christian symbolism for insisting on the monotheistic revolution as cutting loose from that ground, see W. Ong, *Fighting for Life: Contest, Sexuality and Consciousness* (Ithaca: Cornell, 1981), 176f.

30. The imagery in Rev 12 evokes a number of ancient myths of the dragon of chaos attacking the mother and her divine child; see A. Collins, *The Combat Myth in the Book of Revelation* (Missoula: Scholars, 1976).

31. See Perkins, *John*, 224–25.

32. The "nurse" imagery may have been derived from the Cynic philosophers who claimed to heal people's souls; see A. Malherbe, "Gentile as a Nurse: The Cynic Background to 1 Thess ii," *Novum Testamentum* 12 (1970), 203–17.

33. Thompson, *op. cit.*, 203–205.

34. Ong, *op. cit.*

35. *Ibid.*, 51–115.

36. *Ibid.*, 149–52. Ong points out that we do not know what will

result from the psychic pressure being exerted on women to engage in more agonistic forms of behavior: 154f.

37. In so doing, we would run the risk of losing contact with the "psychosomatic" foundations of Christian life and worship; cf. Ong, *op. cit.,* 167–83.

38. *Ibid.,* 193–209. Ong concludes that if consciousness develops out of the unconscious, then we will never be able to fully image the next stage in its development.

39. Ong, *op. cit.,* 178, argues that the overwhelming femininity of the Roman Catholic Church may have called for an all-male clergy as compensation. In "macho cultures," clergy are suspect by other males because of their close association with the feminine Church. He does not intend this observation to settle the question of ordaining women to the priesthood, but only to point out the psychic structures at work in the formation of the present arrangement.

Chapter Five

WOMEN AND ESOTERIC TRADITION IN GNOSTICISM

Introduction

This chapter jumps out of the world of the New Testament into that of the Gnostic sects which challenged orthodox Christianity in the second century.[1] This excursion into the second century is motivated by two claims about Gnostic Christianity which have recently gained attention in non-scholarly circles:[2] (1) that Gnostics envisaged God in a non-patriarchal way as Mother-Father; (2) that Gnostic sects continued the practice of the first-century communities in permitting women to teach, administer sacraments, etc. It is claimed that as orthodox Christianity consolidated power in the bishop, genuine first-century options for women were forced out of the main-line Church into the Gnostic sects.[3] Neither of these positions can be maintained without serious qualifications.[4]

Gnostic systems of divine hierarchy are usually dominated by God as unbegotten Father. Sometimes the highest God is also described as Mother-Father, that is, as androgynous, a common attribute of the divine in this period.[5] Gnostic mythology usually has the female, Sophia (Gk. "wisdom"), as the youngest and weakest of the heavenly aeons which come forth from God. Her instability leads to a fall of light out of the divine world, and, consequently, to the creation of this evil, disordered material world, ruled by Sophia's unfortunate offspring.[6] The souls of Gnostics are divine light which must find its way out of this world to the divine, the *pleroma*. Gnostic ascetics referred to overcoming the ties of passion which bind the soul to the material world as "destroying the works of the female." Since Sophia's plight symbolizes the situation of every soul caught in the material world, the ambivalence surrounding her and "the female" in general in Gnostic writings is not related to sexual distinctions—though sexual passion is to be overcome. It is related to the gulf which separates the embodied soul from the divine world.

The role of women in Gnostic sects is more difficult to discover. Whenever one wished to slander an opponent in antiquity, one could accuse him of appealing only to weak-minded women. Irenaeus makes such charges about the Gnostic teacher Marcus.[7] He claims that Marcus allowed women to celebrate the Eucharist and to prophesy. Even if this evidence were not colored by rhetorical polemic, we cannot push it too far. We have no Gnostic writings which preserve names of any women who were Gnostic teachers with independent groups. Further, the thanksgiving which Irenaeus says Marcus allowed women to pronounce over the cup is performed in his presence. Consequently, the position of women in Gnostic sects was probably not any different from that held in cultic associations generally. They held some roles, prophesied, but were not public representatives of the movement or major teachers.

However, there is a second point about women in Gnostic traditions which is amply documented both in the patristic testimony and in Gnostic writings. The women disciples of Jesus were said to have transmitted esoteric wisdom about the sayings of Jesus. This chain of tradition is also associated with another "outsider" to the original twelve, James, the brother of the Lord. Hippolytus says of the Naasenes: "These are several points out of a great number of discourses which James the Lord's brother is said to have delivered to Mariamne."[8] In the *First Apocalypse of James* (1 ApocJas), Jesus warns James that people will oppose the Gnostic teaching. He tells James to encourage four women: "And when you speak the words of this perception, encourage these four, Salome, Mariam, Martha and Arsinoe."[9] The first three women appear among the disciples who receive esoteric instruction from Jesus in a later Gnostic writing, *Pistis Sophia* (PisSoph).[10] The concluding saying in this section of 1 ApocJas introduces another important theme in the Gnostic sayings tradition. The ascent to immortality makes the female male. Jesus says of his impending ascent to heaven: "The perishable has gone up to the imperishable and the female element has attained to the male element."[11] The reference to making the female male refers to the soul recovering its primordial unity with the divine. It is not concerned with the position of women as opposed to men. All souls which are trapped in this world are female.

Sophia and the Ambiguity of the Female

Sophia appears in Gnostic writings as both virgin and whore. I AM aretalogies play on the ambiguity of her role. The I AM aretalogy is a form of religious expression which was used in the cult of the Egyptian goddess Isis. There, the names and attributes of the goddess are catalogued to show that she is the source of all divinity, of culture and human order. In short, the aretalogy proclaims the benefits which the goddess bestows on humanity. But these praises of Isis are never paradoxical. Scholars have suggested that the paradoxical element in the Gnostic stories of Sophia was based on Jewish speculation about God's wisdom. She is pictured as a divine figure who wanders the earth seeking souls of righteous people in which to make her home. When she is rejected by humans, she returns to the heavenly home from which she came.[12] Gnostic stories expanded the imagery of the wandering Sophia by identifying her with Eve.[13]

In the Jewish tradition, Wisdom (Sophia) is often pictured as with God in the heavens at the creation.[14] The relationship between the Gnostic Sophia and the Mother, who is sometimes the consort of God, is also ambiguous. Sometimes the Mother is active on behalf of humanity, as Wisdom is in the Jewish traditions.[15] In other cases, she stands over against Sophia, since the latter is mired in this world. The identification between Sophia and Eve makes it possible for some Gnostic myths to picture her as a source of enlightenment.[16]

On the Origin of the World (OrigWld) brings together several independent, Gnostic traditions about divine Wisdom, Sophia and Eve into a single account. There are three Adams in this account.[17] There is the heavenly, immortal Light-Adam. That Adam does not belong to this world at all. It is the archetype of true humanity and belongs to the divine world. A vision of that heavenly Adam leads the powers who rule this world and who do not want the light imprisoned here to return to the divine to plan a material copy. Their Adam is to be made in the likeness of the heavenly Adam and in their image.[18] Sophia decides to counteract their plan to keep light imprisoned in the material Adam by creating an intermediate being, the psychic Adam. Like the Immortal Adam, this being is androgynous, Adam-Eve. But it is ambiguous, since it is created both of matter (= watery substance) and out of a drop of light, which belongs to the heavenly world. The powers created the material Adam to be ignorant and enslaved to them. Sophia's psychic Adam, when awakened to knowledge of the divine world through revelation, will master the powers.

When all the light trapped in this world returns to the divine, this world, its God and powers (= the Creator God of Genesis) will all collapse into nothingness.

Identified with this world, Sophia's Adam-Eve is more feminine than masculine. A series of Aramaic puns on the name Eve provide a list of titles for her:[19]

Eve, hwh = hw', "instructor"
          = hy', "life"
          = hyw', "beast"

As Instructor, she calls Adam to receive the spirit. Thus, she brings him to life and is Mother of the Living. As beast, she is identified with the crafty serpent in the tree. The powers seek to rape her, and she escapes by leaving her image to be sexually abused by them. Thus, her image becomes the prostitute over against the virgin Eve.[20] This ambiguity is celebrated in an aretalogy which the author inserts into the myth after the account of the creation of the psychic Adam-Eve:[21]

> Moreover, Eve is the first virgin, since she has no husband. When she gave birth, she healed herself. Therefore, it is said about her that she said:
>   I am the portion of my mother, and I am the mother.
>   I am the woman, and I am the virgin.
>   I am the pregnant one, and I am the physician.
>   I am the midwife.
>   My husband is the one who begot me, and I am his mother.
>   And he is my father and lord.
>   He is my potency. What he desires he speaks with reason.
>   I am still in a nascent state, and I have borne a lordly man.

Another version of the Eve aretalogy appears in the writing which comes before OrigWld in codex two. It is closer to an Isis aretalogy, though it does contain the combination "physician/ one who gives birth." Adam is greeting Eve after she has enlightened him:[22]

> And the spirit-endowed woman came to him and spoke with him, saying, "Arise Adam!" When he saw her, he said: "It is you who have given me life; you will be called Mother of the Living. For it is she who is my mother; it is she who is the physician, and the woman, and she who has given birth."

The more elaborate and more theoretically sophisticated story in OrigWld displays the ambiguous character of the Instructor, Eve-Adam. She constantly works against the powers, but, like humanity, she is caught between this world and the divine. Thus, the paradoxes in the I AM aretalogy are not themselves the means to enlightenment. OrigWld sees salvation as return to the divine, to the androgynous unity of the heavenly Adam. This unity will not be completely achieved until all the light has left this world; this world dissolves, and we are left with the single divine light world out of which everything has come.[23] The relationships between masculine and feminine concern the structure of creation as such. They do not reflect on the division of the material Adam into two sexes. Nor does the image of Eve as Instructor have implications for the position of women as such. She is an androgynous being, an image for all Gnostics.

Patristic writers often accuse the Gnostics of sexual immorality. Some people today have attempted to interpret the paradoxes associated with Eve as a license for indifference to ethical behavior. However, the hints that we find in Gnostic writers about the type of behavior associated with this vision of the world are all ascetic. One writing is a particularly striking example of the combination of paradoxical I AM statements voiced by heavenly Wisdom and the summons to an ascetic life. *Thunder, Perfect Mind* (Thund) opens with a summons to the audience to follow the voice of Wisdom:[24]

> I was sent forth from the power, and I have come to those who reflect on me, and I have been found by those who seek after me. Look upon me, you who reflect upon me, and you, hearers, hear me. You who are waiting for me, take me to yourselves, and do not banish me from your sight. And do not make your voice hate me, nor your hearing. Do not be ignorant of me anywhere or anytime. Be on guard! Do not be ignorant of me!

This summons to follow wisdom is followed by statements of the paradoxical I AM type. The paradoxes will be familiar from the mythological context in OrigWld. They make it clear that this divine voice is not the usual goddess:[25]

> For I am the first and the last.
> I am the honored and the despised one.
> I am the whore and the holy one.
> I am the wife and the virgin.
> I am the mother and the daughter.
> I am the members of my mother.
> I am the barren one, whose sons are many.
> I am she whose wedding is great, and I have not taken
>   a husband.
> I am the solace of my labor pains.
> I am the bride and the bridgroom.
> I am the mother of my father, and the sister of my
>   husband, and he is my offspring.
> But he is the one who begot me before time on a birth
>   day, and he is my offspring in due time.

And my power is from him.
I am the staff of his power in his youth,
and he is the rod of my old age.
And whatever he wills happens to me.

When Wisdom again addresses the audience, she castigates them for their paradoxical reaction to her:[26]

You who hate me, why do you love me,
    and hate those who love me?
You who deny me, confess me,
    and you who confess me, deny me.
You who tell the truth about me, lie about me,
    and you who have lied about me, tell the truth
    about me.
You who know me, be ignorant of me,
    and those who have not known me, let them know
    me.

The rest of Thund continues to alternate aretalogy and address to the audience. It appears that they are called to follow this Wisdom in a situation in which "the wise" are rejecting her. The summons concludes with a call for all who listen to Wisdom to conquer passions and desires:[27]

Look, then, at his words, and all the writings which have been completed. Give heed, you hearers, and you, also, angels, and those who have been sent, and you spirits who have arisen from the dead! For, I am the one who alone exists, and I have no one who will judge me. For, many are the pleasant forms which exist in numerous sins, and incontinencies, and disgraceful passions, and fleeting pleasures, which men embrace until they become sober and go up to their resting place. And they will find me there. And they will live and not die again.

This summons reflects a common topos of Gnostic asceticism. Bodily pleasures keep people chained to the material world, intoxicated. The person who awakens to Gnosis abandons this world for the heavenly one, union with the divine and immortality.

Women and the Sayings Tradition

Another side of Wisdom in antiquity was the tradition of sayings of the wise. Jesus' sayings are understood by Gnostics to be the source of secret wisdom.[28] They claimed that Jesus had instructed his disciples, including women, about the true interpretation of his teaching after the resurrection.[29] Mary Magdalene is the most prominent woman disciple. We also find Salome, Martha, and Mary, the mother of the Lord. Unless a text indicates otherwise, Mary, Mariamme, and Mariam all refer to Magdalene. *Gospel of Philip* (GPhil), commenting on names, says that there were three Marys who "always walked with the Lord"—his mother, her sister, and Magdalene, his companion.[30] Most of these dialogues assume that both the men and women disciples ask questions, receive instruction and are transmitters of the sayings tradition. Some, however, show conflict over the presence and activity of the women. We cannot assume that the reason for the conflict was always the same. Some conflicts may be provoked by orthodox polemics, which insist that tradition handed on through a woman follower cannot be apostolic. Other scenes appear to reflect tensions created by the practice of spiritual interpretation of Jesus' sayings within Gnostic communities.

We have seen that within the first-century Pauline mission some women served as traveling missionaries. By the second century, this practice had been largely abandoned. Even the Gnostic dialogues make it clear that Jesus' male disciples are the ones commissioned to go and preach *gnosis*. Mary (=

Magdalene, unless otherwise indicated) demonstrates her Gnostic insight by instructing them prior to the mission. The *Gospel of Mary* (GMary) has her strengthen them after Jesus' departure:[31]

> But they were grieved. They wept greatly saying, "How shall we go to the Gentiles and preach the gospel of the kingdom of the Son of Man? If they did not spare him, how will they spare us?" Then Mary stood up, greeted them all and said to her brothers, "Do not weep; do not grieve, nor be irresolute, for his grace will be with you and will protect you. But rather let us praise his greatness, for he has prepared us and *made us into men.*" When Mary said this, she turned their hearts to God and they began to discuss the words of the Savior.

In PisSoph, she intervenes with the Lord for further instruction because "my brothers will preach to the whole world."[32] Thus, the male disciples are the ones commissioned to preach the Gnostic gospel, but their understanding of that gospel is, in part, dependent upon insight mediated through the women disciples of Jesus.

Such claims did not go unchallenged. Both GMary and PisSoph contain scenes of conflict between Mary and Peter. They show Peter finally agreeing to the tradition which has come from Jesus through Mary.[33] Peter objects to Mary's account of a private revelation that she has had from the Lord because (1) "these teachings are strange ideas"; (2) why would the Lord have spoken privately to a woman and not to the twelve?[34] However, the disciples finally accept Mary's revelation and go out to preach:[35]

> Then Mary wept and said to Peter, "My brother Peter, what do you think? Do you think that I made this

up myself or that I am lying about the Savior?" Levi answered, saying to Peter, "Peter, you have always been hot-tempered. Now I see you contending against the woman like the adversaries. But if the Savior has made her worthy, who are you to reject her? Surely the Savior knows her very well. That is why he loved her more than us. Rather, let us be ashamed and *put on the perfect man,* and separate as he commanded us and preach the gospel, not laying down any other rule or other law beyond what the Savior said.

The reference to another law or rule beyond what the Savior said may indicate disciplinary action against Gnostic teachers by Church authorities. The *Apocalypse of Peter* (ApocPet) represents such an action as contrary to Petrine authority, since Peter is the founder of Gnostic Christianity.[36] Peter's objections to Mary's interpretations in PisSoph are met with the insistence that any person in whom "the Spirit wells up" has the right to offer an interpretation. Spirit-inspired interpretation is the norm applied to both male and female disciples throughout PisSoph.[37] Peter's eventual acceptance of Jesus' Gnostic teaching is signaled by his pleading for a woman who has done nothing worthy of "the baptisms" rather than condemning her as the Lord had told him.[38] Thus, Peter becomes the antithesis of orthodox Church leaders who were using their (and his) authority against Gnostic teaching.

Not all the conflicts in PisSoph concern the relationship between Gnostics and orthodox opponents. The practice of Spirit-inspired interpretation appears to have created its own conflicts within Gnostic circles. Peter protests that Mary and Salome have been asking so many questions that no one else is getting an opportunity. The Lord tells the women to yield "so that your male brothers may ask questions too."[39] This exchange recalls the problems of ordering spiritual gifts that faced Paul in Corinth, which culminates in a series of rules including that of silencing women (1 Cor 14:33b–36). However, in neither case do the difficulties stem from the gender of those engaged in "Spirit-inspired" speech. PisSoph shows that the problem is the competitiveness and envy that may spring up between members of the community. Thomas complains that, though inspired, he has been afraid to come forward "lest I cause them (= his brothers) to become angry."[40] Philip complains that his responsibility for recording everything does not leave him free to respond to the Spirit and interpret.[41] Another section contains a competitive series of interpretations offered by Mary Magdalene and Mary, the mother of the Lord. This practice is defended by Jesus, "I will not prevent him whose spirit has become understanding, but I urge him the more to speak the thought which has moved him."[42] Thus, we find a familiar set of problems in this third-century Gnostic practice. Spirit-inspired interpretation leads to competition, anger, envy and disputes over who will have the opportunity to speak. Here, Jesus moderates the disputes among his disciples, male and female, without introducing any rules that would limit the freedom of some to speak in the assembly.

Women, Salvation and Becoming Male

We have seen that salvation for the Gnostic can be described as the feminine soul "becoming male" through its union with the divine. The italicized passages in the quotations from GMary show that becoming male and "put on the perfect man" are identical. The disciples, men and women, are true Gnostics. The *Gospel of Thomas* (GTh), logion 114, makes it clear that the transformation is available to women as well as men. Jesus responds to Peter's demand that Mary be excluded, since women are "not worthy of life," by saying, "I myself will lead her to make her male so that she, too, may become a living spirit resembling you males, for every woman who will make herself male will enter the kingdom of Heaven."[43]

Other Gnostic sayings traditions are concerned with "destroying the works of femaleness" as the symbol of the divinizing of the soul. The *Dialogue of the Savior* (DialSav) begins a discussion of this ascent, which includes Mary, Thomas (= Judas) and Matthew, with the injunction, "Pray in the place where there is no female."[44] The works of femaleness are to be destroyed.[45] Sayings about disrobing and not being ashamed belong to the same context. The Gnostic tears off the garments which bind him or her to this world:[46]

> Judas said to Matthew, "We wish to know with what kind of garments we will be clothed, when we come forth from the corruption of the flesh." The Lord said, "The archons and governors have garments that are given to them for a time. As for you, however, since you are sons of truth, you will not be clothed with these temporary garments. Rather, you will be blessed when you strip yourselves, for it is still a great thing . . . outside.

The lost phrase at the end of this passage may equate "stripping" with the unification of opposites, a theme which follows the GTh parallel to this tradition. GTh 22 has that unification expressed as making inside like outside, above like below, male not male and female not female. We have already seen that such formulas of unification have a use in baptismal traditions to express the "new creation" in Christ. Gnostic exegesis has assimilated them to the Gnostic understanding of the soul and its ascent. These traditions also make it clear that despite ascetic hostility to "the works of femaleness," women as a group were not considered inferior in their ability to attain *gnosis.* The division into sexes is one of the elements of mortality, of the earthly Adam, which is to be abandoned in the return to the divine.

Sayings Interpretation, Demonstration of Gnosis

PisSoph has shown that "Spirit-inspired" interpretation was the norm of enlightenment for that community. Anyone who was inspired could offer an interpretation. GMary presents Mary both as the recipient of special revelation from the Lord and the one to encourage the male disciples to take up their mission and interpret Jesus' words. DialSav has her encourage the "brothers" to question Jesus.[47] Other passages in these writings make a special point of confirming Mary's enlightenment as well. She is praised for her questions.[48] She is singled out as a member of an elite group of disciples.[49] She demonstrates her understanding by offering special interpretations of the sayings of the Lord.[50]

Since these dialogues show that both the male and female disciples are enlightened Gnostics, the special place accorded Mary Magdalene does not imply that women as a group have a greater affinity for Gnostic, "Spirit-inspired" interpretation, or that they were the leaders in Gnostic communities. The emphasis defends the tradition of interpreting Jesus' sayings which these Gnostic groups traced back to special disciples of Jesus, Mary Magdalene, Thomas (= Judas) and Matthew. Mary's *gnosis* vindicates the claims made by the Gnostics for the traditions of interpretation which they traced to her.

Summary

The female figures in Gnostic mythology reflect the ambiguities of Gnostic existence in this world. Since the fate of Sophia is the fate of every incarnate soul, the mythic imagery does not make a statement about women as a group. Some Gnostic ascetics may have sought to avoid women in their quest to become free from the passions of the body, but that principle does not appear as a rule. The sayings traditions present women as equally capable of *gnosis*. Both Jesus' men and women disciples become custodians of his sayings. The women are sometimes the first to reach enlightenment. Since they were not apostles, however, the spread of true (= Gnostic) Christianity is left to the male disciples. GMary is our only example of a claim that Gnostic tradition (about the ascent of the soul) goes back to a private revelation to a woman. Even there, Mary's revelation becomes the public property of all the apostles before they go out on the preaching mission to the world. Thus, her revelation is said to belong to the true apostolic tradition.

For all of these traditions, Gnostic enlightenment is demonstrated in the ability to interpret the sayings of Jesus. Since Mary is often shown to be superior to the other disciples in her ability, Gnostic traditions which were said to come from her may be accorded superior status. Anyone who would object to such traditions can only be like Peter, "picking fights with a woman as though she were the enemy." At the same time, this practice could generate internal problems for Gnostic communities just as enthusiasm for spiritual gifts had done in Corinth. Paul introduces rules to limit who may speak and interpret. These rules seem to have been continued within the Pauline churches. However, we do not know what the practices were in early Christianity generally. The transmission of Jesus' sayings remains fluid well into the second century. The practices of intepreting that we meet in Gnostic dialogues may reflect more general patterns of interpretation. However, the hostile exchanges between Mary and Peter do suggest that orthodox Christians were coming to insist that interpretation be tied to "apostolic traditions." Consequently, the Gnostics must present Mary as a genuine witness to that tradition. They insist that "she speaks as a woman who knows the All."

Notes

1. The apologists evidence the severity of the Gnostic challenge in Rome by the mid-second century. One must avoid assuming that they were equally popular elsewhere. Surviving papyri from Egypt suggest a Christianity which was originally formed within the context of Judaism. The break with Judaism in the early second century led to a diffuse movement of Christian groups, among them Gnostics. However, Gnostic influence on a wide scale does not appear until the late second and early third century; see C. Roberts, *Manuscript, Society and Belief in Early Christian Egypt* (London: Oxford, 1979), 49–54; 71f. An English translation of the collection of Coptic, Gnostic writings found near Nag Hammadi in Egypt may be had in J. M. Robinson, ed., *The Nag Hammadi Library in English* (San Francisco: Harper, 1977). Page references to this volume will be given following the abbreviation *NHLE*. The standard system of references refers to the number of the codex in which a writing occurs, then the page and line numbers within that codex. The following abbreviations for the titles of Gnostic writings are used within the body of the chapter:

1 ApocJas = First Apocalypse of James
ApocPet = Apocalypse of Peter
DialSav = Dialogue of the Savior
GMary   = Gospel of Mary
GPhil   = Gospel of Philip
GTh   = Gospel of Thomas
OrigWld = Origin of the World
PisSoph = Pistis Sophia
Thund   = Thunder, Perfect Mind

2. Largely due to the popularization of E. Pagels, *The Gnostic Gospels* (New York: Random House, 1979).
3. Pagels, *op. cit.*, 53–72.
4. See the discussion of E. Fiorenza, "Word, Spirit and Power: Women in Early Christian Communities," *Women of Spirit*, eds. R.

Ruether and E. McLaughlin (New York: Simon & Schuster, 1979), 44–51.

    5. Meeks, *op. cit.,* 183–96.

    6. A devolution from the divine to this world of matter, disorder and imperfection is a common theme in Platonism of the period and should not be invested with all of the negative overtones that Christian dogma ascribes to "the fall"; so J. Dillon, *The Middle Platonists* (London: Duckworth, 1977), 386–89.

    7. Irenaeus, *Adversus Haereses* I 13, 1–5. Marcus is accused of allowing women to pronounce a blessing over the cup (13, 2) and to prophesy (13, 3), and of seducing wealthy women (13, 5).

    8. Hippolytus, *Refutatio* V 7, 1.

    9. CG V 40, 18—41, 7 (NHLE:248).

    10. C. Schmidt and V. MacDermot, *Pistis Sophia* (Leiden: E. J. Brill, 1978).

    11. CG V 41, 15-18 (NHLE:248).

    12. As in 1 Enoch 41, 1-2; see the discussion in G. MacRae, "The Jewish Background of the Gnostic Sophia Myth," *Novum Testamentum* 12 (1970), 88–94.

    13. *Ibid.,* 97–101.

    14. Prov 8:22–31; Wis 7:22—8:1.

    15. She awakens the slumbering Adam in *Apocryphon of John,* CG II 23, 5–8 (NHLE:111); *Trimorphic Protennoia,* CG XIII 45, 3–30 (NHLE:467f).

    16. As in the *Apocalypse of Adam,* CG V 64, 6-30 (NHLE:256f). Eve is the source of *gnosis* for Adam as long as the two are united in one androgynous being; their glory (= gnosis) leaves when the creator god divides them.

    17. The symbolism is derived from the same type of Genesis exegesis that we saw behind the "neither male nor female" formula in Chapter Three. Adam, the image, is immortal, androgynous, the "idea or form" of the human; Adam, the formed, is material, mortal, etc. The Gnostics have found a third category between the two in their exegesis of Genesis.

    18. Another reflection of the double creation account in Genesis.

    19. CG II 113, 30—114, 4 (NHLE:170f).

    20. M. Tardieu, *Trois Mythes Gnostiques* (Paris: Etudes Augustinienes, 1974), 104–107.

    21. CG II 114, 4-15 (NHLE:171).

22. *Nature of the Archons,* CG II 89, 11-17 (NHLE:154).

23. Tardieu, *op. cit.,* 139.

24. CG VI 13, 1-15 (NHLE:271).

25. CG VI 13, 16-14, 9 (NHLE:271f).

26. CG VI 14, 15-25 (NHLE:272).

27. CG VI 21, 12-32 (NHLE:277).

28. Some scholars argue that Gnostic writings evidence the development of an early Wisdom collection of Jesus' sayings different from the collection which developed into the Synoptic sayings tradition; so H. Koester, "Gnostic Writings as Witnesses for the Development of the Sayings Tradition," *The Rediscovery of Gnosticism,* Vol. I (Leiden: E. J. Brill, 1980), 238–61.

29. For a general study of the revelation dialogues between Jesus and his disciples see P. Perkins, *The Gnostic Dialogue* (New York: Paulist, 1980).

30. CG II 59, 6-11 (NHLE:135f).

31. BG 9, 6-24 (NHLE:472).

32. PisSoph III, 114; also II, 88.

33. Other Gnostic traditions show Peter as an enlightened Gnostic teacher; see Perkins, *Dialogue,* 113–30.

34. BG 17, 10-22 (NHLE:473).

35. BG 18, 1-21 (NHLE:473f).

36. CG VII 79, 1—80, 11 (NHLE:343).

37. See PisSoph I, 36, 42; II, 72.

38. PisSoph III, 122.

39. PisSoph IV, 146.

40. PisSoph I, 46.

41. PisSoph I, 42–43. Philip is allowed to interpret, but Jesus answers that Philip, Thomas and Matthew are to record his revelations.

42. PisSoph I, 60–62.

43. Log. 114 (NHLE:130).

44. CG III 144, 13—145, 24 (NHLE:237–38).

45. Compare a logion from the Egyptian gospel quoted in Clement of Alexandria, *Stromata* III ix 63f, "Until when will men die—as long as women give birth. I have come to destroy the works of femaleness."

46. DialSav CG III 143, 11-24 (NHLE:237); cp. GTh Log. 21, which also combines a comment from Mary, parable interpretation and the saying on stripping as this section of DialSav does; GTh 37

(NHLE:121f), and another saying from the Egyptian gospel, Clement of Alexandria, *Stromata* III xiii, 92. See the discussion of these traditions in Koester, *op. cit.,* 254.

47. CG III 131, 19-22 (NHLE:233).

48. PisSoph I, 25; Mary is first to understand, PisSoph I, 17–19.

49. PisSoph II, 96: Mary Magdalene and John, the virgin, are superior to all the disciples; DialSav, CG III 134, 25: Mary, Judas (= Thomas) and Matthew receive a special revelation of the ascent of the soul.

50. DialSav, CG III 139, 8-13 (NHLE:235), ends with "This she spoke as a woman who knows the All": CG III 143, 6-10 (NHLE:237).